Congressional
Research
Service

The President's Office of Science and Technology Policy (OSTP): Issues for Congress

John F. Sargent Jr.
Specialist in Science and Technology Policy

Dana A. Shea
Specialist in Science and Technology Policy

November 26, 2012

Congressional Research Service

7-5700

www.crs.gov

RL34736

CRS Report for Congress ————————————————————————————
Prepared for Members and Committees of Congress

Summary

Congress established the Office of Science and Technology Policy (OSTP) through the National Science and Technology Policy, Organization, and Priorities Act of 1976 (P.L. 94-282). The act states that "The primary function of the OSTP Director is to provide, within the Executive Office of the President [EOP], advice on the scientific, engineering, and technological aspects of issues that require attention at the highest level of Government." Further, "The Office shall serve as a source of scientific and technological analysis and judgment for the President with respect to major policies, plans, and programs of the Federal Government."

The President nominates the OSTP Director, and he is subject to confirmation by the Senate. In many Administrations, the President has concurrently appointed the OSTP Director to the position of Assistant to the President for Science and Technology Policy (APST), a position which allows for the provision of confidential advice to the President on matters of science and technology. President Obama both appointed John Holdren as Assistant to the President for Science and Technology (APST) and nominated him as OSTP Director, a position to which the Senate confirmed him. While Congress can require the OSTP Director to testify, the APST may decline requests to testify on the basis of separation of powers and/or executive privilege. The APST manages the National Science and Technology Council (NSTC), an interagency body established by Executive Order 12881 that coordinates science and technology (S&T) policy across the federal government. The APST also co-chairs the President's Council of Advisors on Science and Technology (PCAST), a council of external advisors established by Executive Order 13539 that provides advice to the President.

In FY2011, Congress sought to restrict OSTP from engaging in certain activities with China or any Chinese-owned company by prohibiting the use of appropriated funds for these activities (P.L. 112-10). The OSTP expended a portion of its FY2011 appropriation to engage in activities with China that Congress sought to proscribe. The Department of Justice and OSTP asserted that this congressional effort infringed upon the President's constitutional authority to conduct foreign diplomacy. In contrast, the Government Accountability Office (GAO) concluded that OSTP violated the Antideficiency Act, though it did not speak to the constitutional issue. Congress enacted a similar restriction for FY2012 (P.L. 112-55) and FY2013 (P.L. 112-175) and may continue its interest in the debate over its ability to restrict the activities of OSTP.

Among other issues Congress may wish to consider are the need for science advice within the EOP; the title, rank, and responsibilities of the OSTP Director; the policy foci of OSTP; the funding and staffing for OSTP; the roles and functions of OSTP and NSTC in setting federal science and technology policy; and the status and influence of PCAST. Some in the S&T community support raising the OSTP Director to cabinet rank, contending that this would imbue the position with more influence within the EOP. Others have proposed that the OSTP Director play a greater role in federal agency coordination, priority-setting, and budget allocation. Both the Administration and Congress have identified areas of policy focus for OSTP staff, raising questions of policy setting and oversight. Some experts say NSTC has insufficient authority over federal agencies engaged in science and technology activities and PCAST insufficient influence on S&T policy; they question the overall coordination of federal science and technology activities. Finally, some in the scientific community support increasing the authority of the OSTP Director in the budget process so as to more strongly influence federal investment in science.

Contents

Figures

Tables

Appendixes

Contacts

Congress established the Office of Science and Technology Policy (OSTP), including the position of its Director, within the Executive Office of the President (EOP) through the National Science and Technology Policy, Organization, and Priorities Act of 1976 (P.L. 94-282) to provide scientific and technological analysis and advice to the President. This codified and institutionalized a presidential science advice function that previously existed at each President's discretion.[1]

This report provides an overview of the history of science and technology (S&T) advice to the President and discusses selected issues and options for Congress regarding OSTP's Director, OSTP management and operations, the President's Council of Advisors on Science and Technology (PCAST), and the National Science and Technology Council (NSTC).

History of Science and Technology Advice to the President

Science and technology policy issues tend to reach the presidential level if they involve multiple agencies; have substantial budgetary, economic, national security, or foreign policy dimensions; are highly controversial (especially those where science and technology matters intersect issues of values, ethics, and morality); or are highly visible to the public. When these matters reach the Oval Office, Presidents generally seek information and advice from trusted sources as to the options and implications of science- and technology-related decisions.

Throughout U.S. history, Presidents have obtained S&T advice through federal scientists and engineers and informal personal contacts.[2] Since the early 1930s, Presidents have attempted to expand their sources of S&T advice through advisory boards and committees. Lacking a statutory foundation, these boards and committees tended to lack permanency, as successive Presidents often disbanded them. When again faced with the need for S&T advice, Presidents would form new advisory boards or committees, sometimes reconstituted from previously disbanded ones.

In the years leading up to World War II, the importance of research and development (R&D) to the nation's economic and military strength became increasingly evident. As a result, President Franklin D. Roosevelt established the Office of Scientific Research and Development (OSRD) in 1941.[3] Historians widely credit the federal R&D enterprise with contributing substantially to the Allied victory in the war, as well as to subsequent U.S. industrial strength. In November 1944, President Roosevelt wrote a letter to OSRD Director Vannevar Bush[4] seeking recommendations

---

[1] This report was originally prepared by former CRS science and technology policy specialist Deborah D. Stine. It has been significantly modified to reflect changes in current policy issues of concern to Congress.

On November 12, 2008, CRS hosted a seminar entitled "The Role of the President's Office of Science and Technology Policy," with outside experts providing different perspectives on OSTP. A video of this seminar is available at http://www.crs.gov/products/multimedia/MM70117.shtml.

[2] For a history of OSTP, see Genevieve J. Knezo, "Science and Technology," Chapter 6 in Harold C. Relyea (ed.), *The Executive Office of the President: A Historical, Biographical, and Bibliographical Guide* (Westport, Connecticut: Greenwood Press, 1997).

[3] President Franklin D. Roosevelt established OSRD within the Office for Emergency Management of the Executive Office of the President. Executive Order 8807, "Establishing the Office of Scientific Research and Development in the Executive Office of the President and Defining Its Functions and Duties," 6 *Federal Register* 3207, July 2, 1941.

[4] OSRD Director Bush reported directly to President Roosevelt.

on how research and the research infrastructure established to support America's war effort could be "profitably employed in times of peace."[5] OSRD Director Bush's response, *Science: The Endless Frontier*,[6] laid out a framework that asserted the essential role of scientific progress in meeting the nation's economic, national security, and social needs. Experts widely view it as foundational to today's U.S. science and technology policy. Among its recommendations, the report asserted:

> The Federal Government should accept new responsibilities for promoting the creation of new scientific knowledge and the development of scientific talent in our youth.[7]

The next several Presidents used a variety of mechanisms to obtain S&T advice within the EOP, to enhance interagency coordination, and to receive counsel from outside advisors. Organizations within the EOP included the Office of the Special Assistant to the President for Science and Technology (Eisenhower) and the Office of Science and Technology (OST; Kennedy, Johnson). Examples of organizations focused on interagency coordination included the President's Scientific Research Board (Truman), the Federal Council for Science and Technology (FCST; Eisenhower, Kennedy, Johnson, Nixon), and the Federal Coordinating Council for Science, Engineering, and Technology (FCCSET; Ford, Carter, Reagan, George H.W. Bush). Examples of external advisory committees included the Science Advisory Committee (Truman, Eisenhower), and the President's Science Advisory Committee (PSAC; Eisenhower, Kennedy, Johnson).

President Nixon abolished the Office of Science and Technology—the S&T policy office then extant in the Executive Office of the President (EOP). The National Science Foundation (NSF) assumed its civilian functions and the National Security Council (NSC) its security functions.[8] In addition, President Nixon opted not to appoint new members to PSAC after accepting the pro forma resignation of its members.[9] President Ford supported the return of a science advisory mechanism to the White House, but he wished to establish it through legislation, not executive order.[10] He signed the National Science and Technology Policy, Organization, and Priorities Act of 1976 (P.L. 94-282) into law on May 11, 1976. This act established OSTP and the position of OSTP Director.

Policy tensions and power struggles between OSTP and other EOP offices and between presidential administrations and the science community are not new. Carter Administration OSTP Director Frank Press, for example, battled the Council on Environmental Quality (CEQ), opposing the CEQ-advocated use of federal subsidies to the then-infant solar power industry and

---

[5] Letter from President Franklin D. Roosevelt to Vannevar Bush, Director, Office of Scientific Research and Development, November 17, 1944, http://www.nsf.gov/od/lpa/nsf50/vbush1945.htm#letter.

[6] Vannevar Bush, Science The Endless Frontier: A Report to the President by Vannevar Bush, Director of the Office of Scientific Research and Development, Office of Scientific Research and Development, Executive Office of the President, Washington, DC, July 5, 1945, http://www.nsf.gov/od/lpa/nsf50/vbush1945.htm#ch1.

[7] Ibid. The report asserted that a shortage of university-educated scientists and engineers resulted from the diversion of college-age students to the war effort created the need for a program to support the development of scientists and engineers.

[8] David Z. Beckler, "The Precarious Life of Science in the White House," *Daedalus*, vol. 103, no. 3 (Summer 1974), p. 115, http://www.jstor.org/stable/20024223.

[9] Ibid.

[10] Jeffrey K. Stine, *A History of Science Policy in the United States, 1940-1985*, Report for the House Committee on Science and Technology Task Force on Science Policy, 99th Cong., 2nd sess., Committee Print (Washington, DC: GPO, 1986), http://ia341018.us.archive.org/2/items/historyofscience00unit/historyofscience00unit.pdf.

---

instead supporting a balanced pace between market demand and scientific discovery.[11] In July 1981, George Keyworth, Reagan Administration OSTP Director, stirred controversy in the science community with his first speech to the American Association for the Advancement of Science (AAAS) by asserting "Nowhere is it indicated that the OSTP or its director is to represent the interests of the scientific community as a constituency." Further, he added that serving as an "inside lobbyist" for the science community would work against the community's interest by reducing his influence within the White House.[12] Keyworth's view of the role of the President's science advisor was at odds with many in the science community at that time. During the George H.W. Bush Administration, tension existed between OSTP Director D. Allan Bromley and other high-ranking White House officials over the extent of Administration support for federal funding of commercial technology development. These tensions became public when the *Wall Street Journal* published articles asserting Bromley's success in advancing an industrial policy in the Administration, including "picking technological winners and losers."[13] Following criticism from Michael Boskin, Chairman of the Council of Economic Advisors (CEA); White House Chief of Staff John Sununu; and OMB Director Richard Darman, Bromley issued a statement clarifying that the Administration's "principles are inconsistent with an industrial policy of targeting particular industries for support or particular technologies for commercialization."[14]

The Appendix provides a historical compilation of presidential S&T policy advisors with their titles, EOP S&T agencies/offices, interagency coordination organizations, and advisory committees. As illustrated in **Table A-1**, the Presidents subsequent to President Ford continued to adapt OSTP and related organizations to suit their needs. For example, P.L. 112-282 included provisions for the OSTP Director to chair an Intergovernmental Science, Engineering, and Technology Advisory Panel (ISETAP). An executive branch, cabinet-level council established by presidential Executive Order, the National Science and Technology Council, which is chaired by the President and managed by the OSTP Director, has subsumed ISETAP's responsibilities. In addition, P.L. 94-282 also established a President's Committee on Science and Technology (PCST) with the OSTP Director as a member. The PCAST largely assumed the role of PCST with the OSTP Director serving as a co-chair along with one or two nonfederal PCAST members.[15]

Overview of OSTP

Congress established the Office of Science and Technology Policy as an office within the EOP to, among other things, "serve as a source of scientific and technological analysis and judgment for the President with respect to major policies, plans, and programs of the Federal Government."[16]

---

[11] David Dickson, *The New Politics of Science* (NY: Pantheon Books/Random House, Inc., 1984), pp. 37-38.

[12] Barbara J. Culliton, "Keyworth Gives First Speech," *Science*, July 7, 1981, pp. 183-184.

[13] Bob Davis, "White House, Reversing Policy Under Pressure, Begins to Pick High-Tech Winners and Losers," *Wall Street Journal*, May 13, 1991, p. A16; Bob Davis, "White House Tries to Distance Itself from Panel Report," *Wall Street Journal*, April 26, 1991, p. A16.

[14] "Bush Science Aide Issues a Statement to Quell Criticism," *Wall Street Journal*, May 17, 1991, p. A11.

[15] Executive Order 12700 first established PCAST (Executive Order 12700, "President's Council of Advisors on Science and Technology," 55 *Federal Register* 2219, January 23, 1990). Executive Order 13539 most recently reestablished PCAST (Executive Order 13539, "President's Council of Advisors on Science and Technology," 75 *Federal Register* 21973-21975, April 27, 2010, http://edocket.access.gpo.gov/2010/pdf/2010-9796.pdf).

[16] P.L. 94-282.

Within the context of its organic statute, OSTP currently defines its mission as having three components:

- Provide the President and his senior staff with accurate, relevant, and timely scientific and technical advice on all matters of consequence.

- Ensure that the policies of the Executive Branch are informed by sound science.

- Ensure that the scientific and technical work of the Executive Branch is properly coordinated so as to provide the greatest benefit to society.[17]

To this end, OSTP has established the following strategic goals and objectives:

- Ensure that federal investments in science and technology are making the greatest possible contribution to economic prosperity, public health, environmental quality, and national security.

- Energize and nurture the processes by which government programs in science and technology are resourced, evaluated, and coordinated.

- Sustain the core professional and scientific relationships with government officials, academics, and industry representatives that are required to understand the depth and breadth of the Nation's scientific and technical enterprise, evaluate scientific advances, and identify potential policy proposals.

- Generate a core workforce of world-class expertise capable of providing policy-relevant advice, analysis, and judgment for the President and his senior staff regarding the scientific and technical aspects of the major policies, plans, and programs of the federal government.[18]

The OSTP also has several unarticulated roles, including serving as a sounding board and conduit of information for agency executives seeking to understand, clarify, and help shape policy objectives and priorities on science and technology-related matters; helping agencies coordinate and integrate their S&T strategies and activities; and helping resolve agency conflicts over areas of responsibility and leadership in S&T fields and related policies.

The role and influence of OSTP, NSTC, PCAST, and its predecessor organizations have varied among Administrations, depending on the President, the individual serving as OSTP Director, and the rapport between them.[19] The following sections provide an overview of the current responsibilities and roles of the OSTP Director and Associate Directors, NSTC, and PCAST, followed by information on OSTP's budget and staffing.

Roles of the OSTP Director/APST and Associate Directors

P.L. 94-282 establishes the position of OSTP Director whose primary function is "to provide, within the Executive Office of the President, advice on the scientific, engineering, and

---

[17] OSTP, "About OSTP," http://www.whitehouse.gov/administration/eop/ostp/about.

[18] Ibid.

[19] For a discussion of the varying influence accorded Science Advisers, listen to National Public Radio, *The Evolving Role of the Presidential Science Advisor*, Talk of the Nation, November 16, 2007, http://www.npr.org/templates/story/story.php?storyId=16343713.

technological aspects of issues that require attention at the highest level of Government." In addition, the OSTP Director is to:

- advise the President of scientific and technological considerations involved in areas of national concern including, but not limited to, the economy, national security, homeland security, health, foreign relations, the environment, and the technological recovery and use of resources;

- evaluate the scale, quality, and effectiveness of the federal effort in science and technology and advise on appropriate actions;

- advise the President on scientific and technological considerations with regard to federal budgets, assist the Office of Management and Budget (OMB) with an annual review and analysis of funding proposed for R&D in budgets of all federal agencies, and aid the OMB and the agencies throughout the budget development process; and

- assist the President in providing general leadership and coordination of the R&D programs of the federal Government.[20]

By statute, the President appoints the OSTP Director, who is sometimes referred to colloquially as the President's science advisor.[21] The OSTP Director is subject to Senate confirmation and receives compensation at the rate provided for level II of the Executive Schedule. The OSTP Director has never been a member of the President's Cabinet or a cabinet-level official.

In addition to establishing the position of OSTP Director, P.L. 94-282 authorizes the President to appoint not more than four OSTP Associate Directors, subject to Senate confirmation, who are compensated at a rate not to exceed that provided for level III of the Executive Schedule. The number of Associate Director positions has varied under different Presidents. For example, under President George W. Bush there were two OSTP Associate Directors—one focused on science and the other on technology—each with a Deputy Director.[22] During the Clinton Administration, four Associate Directors focused on science; technology; environment; and national security and international affairs issues. President Obama has established four OSTP Associate Director positions with discrete areas of responsibility: environment and energy, national security and international affairs, science, and technology. (The section below, "Number and Policy Foci of OSTP Associate Directors," provides a more detailed discussion of the role of OSTP Associate Directors.)

Presidential Appointment Status and Congress

The formal positions held by the President's science advisor may affect their degree of access to the President and other EOP decision makers. (See **Appendix** for a historical overview of science advisors and their titles.) Although Presidents have differed in their management of EOP staff,

---

[20] P.L. 94-282.

[21] While there is no statutory EOP title or position of "Science Advisor" or "Presidential Science Advisor," this term is often used to describe the individual serving as the primary advisor to the President on science and technology issues. Executive Order 13539 states that the Assistant to the President for Science and Technology (APST) is equivalent to the "Science Advisor" and shall serve as a co-chair of PCAST; the position of PCAST co-chair is currently held by APST/OSTP Director John Holdren.

[22] Based on CRS discussions with Stanley Sokul, Chief of Staff, Bush Administration OSTP, August 14, 2008.

Cabinet members and assistants to the President generally have greater access to the President than other White House staff.[23]

Some members of the S&T policy community question the degree of presidential access available to the OSTP Director. The OSTP Director is not a cabinet-level official. Some Presidents have appointed their science advisors, however, not only to the Senate-confirmed position of OSTP Director, but also as Assistant to the President for Science and Technology (APST). These positions do not require Senate confirmation and may confer additional status and access to the President. While President Obama appointed John Holdren to serve as both Director of OSTP and APST, President George W. Bush appointed John Marburger only to the position of OSTP Director; President Bush did not appoint an APST during his two terms.

The relationship between Congress and the individual serving as the President's science advisor varies depending on whether the individual serves as OSTP Director, APST, or both. Congress can require the OSTP Director to testify before Congress; APSTs may assert the right not to testify before Congress in accordance with the principles of separation of powers and/or executive privilege.[24] There may be ambiguity about Congress's authority to require testimony from an individual who holds both the Director of OSTP and APST title, depending on the capacity in which the individual would testify and the subject matter of the testimony.

Roles and Responsibilities

Historically, the OSTP Director advises the President on policy formulation; presidential appointments; S&T-related budget issues, including R&D; the policy significance of scientific and technical developments; and science, technology, engineering, and mathematics (STEM) education.[25] OSTP Directors historically have served as communication conduits between the EOP and the federal and non-federal S&T community. Some OSTP Directors have emphasized communicating the views of the S&T community to the EOP, while others have focused on communicating the views of the EOP to the S&T community.

The OSTP Director (when serving as APST) also manages the National Science and Technology Council, established by Executive Order 12881,[26] which is charged with coordinating S&T policy across the federal government, establishing national goals for federal S&T investments, and preparing coordinated R&D strategies. As NSTC manager, the OSTP Director/APST can provide federal agency coordination, information, and guidance when special events occur, such as national emergencies, disasters, or S&T-related international negotiations.

---

[23] Information on the President's cabinet is available at http://www.whitehouse.gov/government/cabinet.html.

[24] For a fuller discussion of this issue, see CRS Report RL31351, *Presidential Advisers' Testimony Before Congressional Committees: An Overview*, by Todd Garvey, Alissa M. Dolan, and Henry B. Hogue.

[25] Based on Carnegie Commission on Science, Technology, and Government, *Science & Technology and the President* (New York: Carnegie Corporation of New York, October 1988); National Academies, *Science and Technology Advice in the White House: Recommendations for President-Elect George Bush* (Washington, DC: National Academy Press, 1988); and National Academies, Committee on Science, Engineering, and Public Policy, *Science and Technology for America's Progress: Ensuring the Best Presidential Appointments in the New Administration* (Washington, DC: National Academy Press, 2008), http://www.nap.edu/catalog.php?record_id=12481.

[26] Executive Order 12881, "Establishment of the National Science and Technology Council," 58 *Federal Register* 62491-62492, November 23, 1993, http://www.archives.gov/federal-register/executive-orders/pdf/12881.pdf.

In addition, the OSTP Director (when also serving as APST) co-chairs the President's Council of Advisors on Science and Technology, established by Executive Order 13226.[27] As co-chair of PCAST, the OSTP Director/APST can ascertain the consensus of the S&T community on issues of interest to the Administration.

Under Executive Order 12472, the OSTP Director performs some special roles regarding National Security Emergency Preparedness communications.[28] First, Section 706 of the Communications Act (47 U.S.C. 151 et seq.) designates the OSTP Director to exercise most of the President's wartime telecommunications authorities.[29] In general, performance of these presidentially delegated functions requires a Senate-confirmed OSTP Director.[30] Second, under Executive Order 12472, the OSTP Director also exercises several non-wartime emergency telecommunications functions and leads the interagency Joint Telecommunications Resources Board (JTRB). The JTRB provides a forum for top-level discussions of emergency communications issues during times of crisis. In the wake of the September 11, 2001, terrorist attacks, Bush Administration OSTP Director John Marburger designated one civil service staff member to support continuity on these issues across presidential administrations.[31] This approach has continued through the Obama Administration.[32]

---

[27] Executive Order 13226, "President's Council of Advisors on Science and Technology," 66 *Federal Register* 50523-52524, October 3, 2001, http://frwebgate.access.gpo.gov/cgi-bin/getdoc.cgi?dbname=2001_register&docid=fr03oc01-141.pdf.

[28] Executive Order 12472, "Assignment of National Security and Emergency Preparedness Telecommunications Functions," 49 *Federal Register* 13471; April 5, 1984; http://www.ncs.gov/library/policy_docs/eo_12472.html.

[29] Under the Communications Act, the federal government can direct commercial telecommunications companies to perform specific functions, such as providing priority services, on its behalf.

[30] An exception exists for an official serving as the Acting Director through a Presidentially approved succession order.

[31] Based on CRS discussions with Stanley Sokul, Chief of Staff, OSTP, November 6, 2008.

[32] Based on communication from Rachael Leonard, General Counsel, OSTP, January 24, 2012.

Figure I. Office of Science and Technology Policy Organization

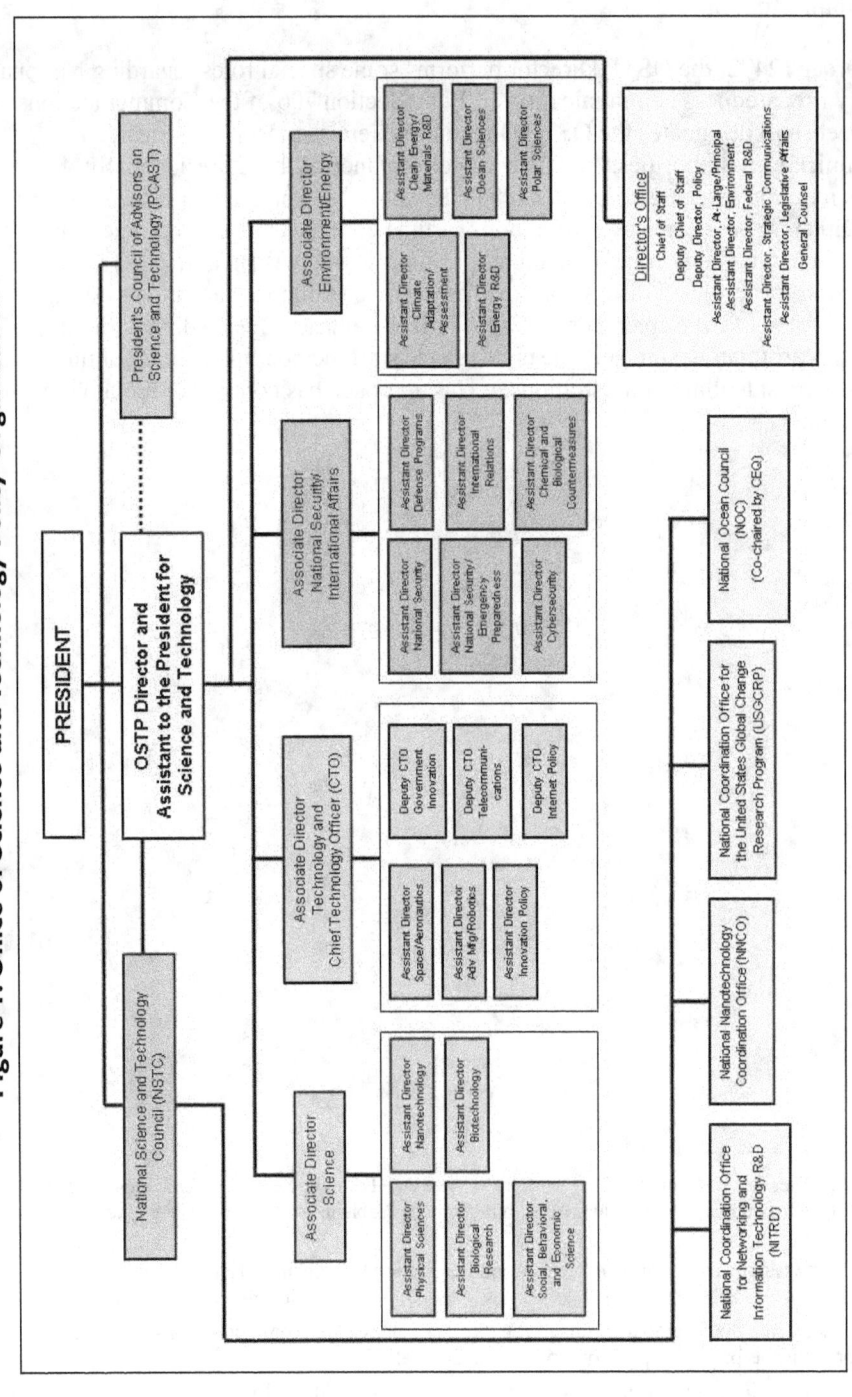

Source: Congressional Research Service based on information in OSTP, "Leadership and Staff," at http://www.ostp.gov/cs/about_ostp/leadership_staff. The organization chart has been reviewed and approved by OSTP via personal communication with CRS on February 3, 2012.

Notes: This chart is subject to change as appointments are made by the President. The Associate Director of Technology and the Associate Director of Environment have been nominated and confirmed by the Senate. The other Associate Director positions have not been nominated, but the OSTP Director has indicated the intention of OSTP including Associate Directors with these titles during congressional testimony. Each Associate Director is in charge of a division with the same name with the exception of the Associate Director for Environment who is in charge of the Energy and Environment Division. For more information on the open government initiative, see http://www.whitehouse.gov/open/.

Relationship with Other Agencies

The OSTP Director does not have direct authority over federal agencies or the Office of Management and Budget. The OSTP interacts with other agencies through two principal mechanisms: management of the NSTC and participation with OMB in the budget development process. The following section, "

National Science and Technology Council," discusses OSTP's role in the NSTC. The OSTP's participation with OMB in the budget process involves four basic steps: (1) overall priority setting by OSTP and OMB, (2) agency preparation of budget proposal to OMB, (3) agency negotiations with OMB, and (4) final budget decision by the President and OMB Director.

A key activity in the first step is OSTP's request to federal agencies for their recommendations on R&D priorities. In addition, interagency working groups meet to determine individual agency responsibility for certain activities where multiple agencies share responsibility for a given issue area. The OSTP and OMB use this information as the basis for a joint memorandum that describes the Administration's R&D priorities and R&D investment criteria.[33] Agencies are to use this memorandum as an aid in the second step, preparation of their budgets.

During the second step, agencies prepare their budgets. The OSTP continually interacts with the agencies, providing advice and working with them on their priorities. In general, OSTP gives more guidance to agencies with large R&D budgets and to programs that cross agency boundaries. Once completed, federal agencies then submit their proposed budgets to OMB. The OSTP does not review proposed agency budgets before they are sent to OMB.

In the third step, OSTP works with OMB to review the proposed budgets to see if they reflect Administration plans and priorities. The OSTP also participates in OMB budget examiner presentations to the OMB Director and provides advice on priorities at that time. In addition, OSTP provides direct feedback to agencies as they negotiate with OMB over funding levels and the programs on which that funding is to be spent.

OSTP's primary role in the fourth step in the budget process is to advise on the quality of the proposals and their relevance to the established priorities. The President, the OMB Director, and the Cabinet however make the ultimate choices.

---

[33] The OMB and OSTP did not issue a joint memorandum on Administration R&D priorities and investment criteria for FY2013 but instead jointly conveyed informal guidance on R&D priorities to federal departments and agencies. Further, OSTP asserted that the formal OSTP-OMB R&D priorities guidance memo was not issued for the FY2013 budget due to "unusual delays in the budget formulation process for FY2013 resulting from negotiations and enactment of the Budget Control Act in August 2011." E-mail communication from OSTP General Counsel Rachael Leonard to CRS, January 24, 2012. The OMB and OSTP issued a joint science and technology priorities memorandum for FY2014 on June 6, 2012. Jeffrey D. Zients, Acting Director, Office of Management and Budget, and John P. Holdren, Director, Office of Science and Technology Policy, "Science and Technology Priorities for the FY2014 Budget," *Memorandum for the Heads of Executive Departments and Agencies*, June 6, 2012.

National Science and Technology Council

On November 23, 1993, President Clinton established the National Science and Technology Council (NSTC) by Executive Order (EO) 12881.[34] The NSTC is a principals council that also contains selected assistants and advisers to the President. The APST is specified in EO 12881 as a member of the NSTC; the OSTP Director is not. The NSTC aims to coordinate science and technology policy across the federal government. According to the executive order, NSTC has the following principal functions:

- Coordinate the S&T policymaking process.

- Ensure S&T policy decisions and programs are consistent with the President's stated goals.

- Help integrate the President's S&T policy agenda across the federal government.

- Ensure science and technology are considered in development and implementation of federal policies and programs.

- Further international cooperation in science and technology.

In addition to these principal functions, the NSTC assists the OMB Director by recommending R&D budgets that reflect national goals and advising on agency R&D submissions.

The OSTP Director chaired the NSTC's predecessor, the Federal Coordinating Council for Science, Engineering, and Technology (FCCSET). In contrast, the President chairs the NSTC; in the President's absence, the Vice President or the APST serves as chair. In practice, the NSTC rarely meets with the President or cabinet-level officials present. Rather, OSTP staff and detailees[35] manage NSTC activities in conjunction with federal agency staff.

The NSTC has five primary committees: Science; Technology; Environment, Natural Resources, and Sustainability; Homeland and National Security; and Science, Technology, Engineering, and Math Education. As shown in **Table 1**, each NSTC committee has subcommittees, interagency working groups, and/or taskforces focused on specialized topics. The members of these committees and subcommittees are generally not cabinet officials, but instead lower-ranking staff.

The NSTC also may undertake certain responsibilities to meet congressional mandates. For example, the America COMPETES Act (P.L. 110-69) directs the establishment of a President's Council on Innovation and Competitiveness. The act states that the council is to include the Secretary or head of a number of federal agencies, OSTP, and OMB. Rather than establish a new, independent council, President George W. Bush assigned this responsibility to the NSTC Committee on Technology.[36]

---

[34] Executive Order 12881, "Establishment of the National Science and Technology Council," 58 *Federal Register* 62491-62492, November 23, 1993. The executive order also states that NSTC oversees the duties of the Federal Coordinating Council for Science, Engineering, and Technology (FCCSET), the National Space Council, and the National Critical Materials Council, none of which have met since creation of the NSTC.

[35] A detail is an officially approved temporary assignment of a civil service employee (informally called a "detailee") to a different position in another federal agency. The employee's official title, series, grade, rate of compensation, and permanent employer does not change.

[36] Memorandum of the President of the United States, "Designation of the Committee on Technology of the National Science and Technology Council to Carry out Certain Requirements of the America COMPETES Act," 73 *Federal* (continued...)

Congress has charged the NSTC with specific statutory responsibilities. Congress mandated the NSTC to coordinate federal activities on ocean acidification[37] and develop an implementation plan for a coordinated national research program on the role of the oceans in human health and to annually report on these activities.[38] Congress also directed the NSTC to oversee the planning, management, and coordination of the National Nanotechnology Program and annually report on these activities.[39] In addition, Congress directed the OSTP Director to establish a NSTC committee with the responsibility to coordinate federal programs and activities in support of STEM education,[40] to establish a committee responsible for planning and coordinating federal programs and activities in advanced manufacturing research and development,[41] to establish a working group responsible for coordinating federal science agency research and policies related to the dissemination and long-term stewardship of the results of unclassified research,[42] and to use the NSTC to annually identify and prioritize deficiencies in federal research facilities and major instrumentation.[43]

President's Council of Advisors on Science and Technology

The President's Council of Advisors on Science and Technology (PCAST) advises the President, both directly and through the APST, on science, technology, and innovation policy. In addition, it responds to requests for advice from the National Science and Technology Council. President George H.W. Bush originally created PCAST.[44] Presidents Clinton, George W. Bush, and Obama reestablished slightly different versions of PCAST during their administrations.[45]

The current executive order provides PCAST a broad remit, stating that its advice "shall include, but not be limited to, policy that affects science, technology, and innovation, as well as scientific and technical information that is needed to inform public policy relating to the economy, energy, environment, public health, national and homeland security, and other topics." The PCAST also serves as two other statutorily created advisory committees: the President's Innovation and Technology Advisory Committee created by the High Performance Computing Act of 1991 (P.L. 102-94 as amended) and the National Nanotechnology Advisory Panel created by the 21st Century Nanotechnology Research and Development Act (P.L. 108-153).

(...continued)

Register 20523, April 10, 2008.

[37] P.L. 111-11, "The Omnibus Public Land Management Act of 2009," §12403.

[38] P.L. 108-447, div. B, title IX, "Oceans and Human Health Act," §902.

[39] P.L. 108-153, §2, "21st Century Nanotechnology Research and Development Act."

[40] P.L. 111-358, "America COMPETES Reauthorization Act of 2010," §101.

[41] P.L. 111-358, "America COMPETES Reauthorization Act of 2010," §102.

[42] P.L. 111-358, "America COMPETES Reauthorization Act of 2010," §103.

[43] P.L. 110-69, "America COMPETES Act," §1007.

[44] Executive Order 12700, "President's Council of Advisors on Science and Technology," 55 *Federal Register* 2219, January 23, 1990.

[45] Clinton Administration: Executive Order 12882, "President's Committee of Advisors on Science and Technology," 58 *Federal Register* 62492-62493, November 26, 2003; George W. Bush Administration: Executive Order 13226, "President's Council of Advisors on Science and Technology," 66 *Federal Register* 50523-50524, October 3, 2001; Obama Administration: Executive Order 13539, "President's Council of Advisors on Science and Technology," 75 *Federal Register* 21973-21975, April 27, 2010.

Table 1. National Science and Technology Council Committees

COMMITTEE ON ENVIRONMENT, NATURAL RESOURCES, AND SUSTAINABILITY (CENRS)		
AQRS: Air Quality Research (SC)	[Proposed] RCIS: Roundtable on Climate Information & Services (WG)	SWAQ: Water Availability & Quality (SC)
CSMSC: Critical & Strategic Mineral Supply Chain (SC)	SDR: Disaster Reduction (SC)	T&R: Toxics and Risk (SC)
[Proposed]: IARPC: Interagency Arctic Research Policy Committee (IWG)	SES: Ecological Services (SC)	USGEO: U.S. Group on Earth Observations (SC)
[Proposed] ISTS: Integration of Science and Technology for Sustainability (TF)	SGCR: Global Change Research (SC)	
NEO: National Earth Observations (TF)	SOST: Ocean Science & Technology (SC)	

COMMITTEE ON HOMELAND AND NATIONAL SECURITY (CHNS)		
CDRD: Chemical Defense R&D (SC)	HS S&T: Homeland Security S&T Policy (TF)	[Proposed] SCIST: International Science, Engineering & Technology (SC)
D-IED: Domestic IEDs (SC)	SOS_CBRNE: Standards (SC)	
BDRD: Biological Defense R&D (SC)	ISC: Infrastructure (SC)	
HFHNS: Human Factors for Homeland and National Security (SC)	NDRD: Nuclear Defense R&D (SC)	

COMMITEE ON SCIENCE (CoS)		
DDWG: Digital Data (IWG)	PASP: Public Access to Scholarly Publications (TF)	SBE: Social, Behavioral, & Economic Science (SC)
LSSC: Life Science (SC)	PSSC: Physical Science (SC)	SoSF: Forensic Science (SC)
Aquaculture (IWG)	Scientific Collections (IWG)	Quantum Information Science (IWG)
Research Business Models (IWG)	Science of Sound Policy (IWG)	TF A-21: Cost Principles for Educational Institutions

COMMITTEE ON STEM EDUCATION (CoSTEM)		
FC-STEM: Federal Coordination in STEM Education (TF)	FI-STEM: Federal Investment in STEM Education (FTAC)	

COMMITTEE ON TECHNOLOGY (CoT)		
ASTS: Aeronautics Science & Technology (SC)	IAM: Advanced Manufacturing (IWG)	SG: Smart Grid (SC)
BidM: Biometrics and Identity Management (SC)	NITRD: Networking & Information Technology Research & Development (SC)	SoS: Standards (SC)
BTRD: Building Technology R&D (SC)	NSET: Nanoscale Science, Engineering, and Technology (SC)	TFSD: Smart Disclosure (TF)
H2FC: Hydrogen & Fuel Cells (IWG)	P2I: Privacy and Internet Policy (SC)	

Source: National Science and Technology Council, website, accessed January 10, 2012, at http://www.ostp.gov/cs/nstc/committees.

Notes: SC = subcommittee; IWG = interagency working group; TF = task force.

PCAST's members include approximately 20-25 distinguished individuals from industry, education and research institutions, and other organizations outside the federal government. The APST co-chairs PCAST along with one or two other council members. Until recently, OSTP provided funding and support for PCAST. Now, President Obama has directed the Department of Energy to provide PCAST with funding and administrative and technical support.[46]

According to OSTP, though the funding, administrative, and technical support functions for PCAST were transferred from OSTP to DOE in December 2011, OSTP continues to exercise policy and programmatic oversight of PCAST through co-chair John Holdren and PCAST's staff, who continue to be physically located at OSTP. The OSTP expects that PCAST's funding level at DOE will be comparable to PCAST's historic funding levels at OSTP, noting that Congress has not provided additional appropriations to DOE specifically to support PCAST.[47]

OSTP Budget and Staffing

OTSP's budget and staffing relates, in part, to the degree OSTP can provide advice to the President and respond to congressional action. **Figure 2** provides OSTP's budget levels and **Figure 3** provides OSTP's staffing levels from FY1977 until FY2012. The OSTP's FY2012 budget is $4.5 million, $1.5 million less than in FY2011.[48] The Obama Administration, through the NSF budget, received an additional $3.14 million for FY2012 to support OSTP's federally funded research and development center (FFRDC), the Science and Technology Policy Institute (STPI; see box below). The continuing resolution for FY2013 provides effectively equal funding for OSTP in FY2013 as in FY2012.[49]

As illustrated in **Figure 2** and **Figure 3**, OSTP funding and staffing levels have varied among presidential administrations. In constant dollars, OSTP funding was at its highest during the George H.W. Bush Administration and at its lowest during the Reagan Administration. OSTP's staffing also fluctuated, generally increasing since the beginning of the G.H.W. Bush Administration. Some analysts have expressed concern that the uneven funding and staffing of OSTP may result in inconsistent provision of S&T advice within the EOP over time.

The OSTP possesses 40 full-time equivalent staff positions. As of February 2012, OSTP had a total of 92 staff members, detailees, fellows, and those on an Intergovernmental Personnel Agreement (IPAs).[50] According to OSTP, this total includes 10 political staff, 17 career staff, 1 consultant, 49 detailees, 9 IPAs and 6 fellows.[51] Political staff, career staff, and consultants are funded by OSTP; detailees are funded by their home agencies; fellows are funded by a variety of

---

[46] Executive Order 13596, "Amendments to Executive Orders 12131 and 13539," 76 *Federal Register* 80725-80726, December 27, 2011.

[47] E-mail communication from OSTP General Counsel Rachael Leonard to CRS, January 24, 2012.

[48] Ongoing controversy about OSTP compliance with statutory restrictions on the expenditure of appropriated funds underlie the reduction in OSTP FY2012 appropriations relative to FY2011. For more information, see "OSTP Compliance with Statutory Restrictions on the Use of Appropriated Funds" later in the report.

[49] Continuing Appropriations Resolution, 2013 (P.L. 112-175) provides funding for OSTP and other federal agencies through March 27, 2013.

[50] E-mail communication from OSTP General Counsel Rachael Leonard to CRS, February 1, 2012.

[51] Fellows are scientists and engineers who come to Washington, DC, to gain experience in public policy. Most are recent graduates of doctoral programs, but some are more experienced staff from industry or universities. Fellows generally come for a year, but that time can be extended.

organizations; and IPAs may be funded by OSTP, their home agencies/organizations, or a combination of the two.[52]

Science and Technology Policy Institute

The Science and Technology Policy Institute (STPI) is a federally funded research and development center (FFRDC) that provides analytical support to the Office of Science and Technology Policy. Congress created STPI through P.L. 101-510. This law established the Critical Technologies Institute (CTI), an FFRDC under the sponsorship of OSTP but supported by appropriations provided to the Department of Defense (DOD). The RAND Corporation initially managed CTI.

In 1998, Congress enacted the National Science Foundation Authorization Act of 1998 (P.L. 105-207), which changed the organization's name to the Science and Technology Policy Institute, changed primary sponsorship to the National Science Foundation, and amended its duties.

In 2003, the Institute for Defense Analysis (IDA) was selected to manage STPI. NSF appropriations provide funding for STPI, including \$3.14 million in FY2012 and \$3.04 million in FY2011. The STPI has up to approximately 30-40 full-time employees.[a] The STPI may also contract for expertise as required for a particular project.[b] In addition, STPI has access to the expertise of IDA's approximately 800 other employees.

The duties of STPI, as specified in 42 U.S.C. 6686, include:

(1) The assembly of timely and authoritative information regarding significant developments and trends in science and technology research and development in the United States and abroad.

(2) Analysis and interpretation of the information referred to in paragraph (1) with particular attention to the scope and content of the federal science and technology research and development portfolio as it affects interagency and national issues.

(3) Initiation of studies and analysis of alternatives available for ensuring the long-term strength of the United States in the development and application of science and technology, including appropriate roles for the Federal Government, State governments, private industry, and institutions of higher education in the development and application of science and technology.

(4) Provision, upon the request of the Director of the Office of Science and Technology Policy, of technical support and assistance -

(A) to the committees and panels of the President's Council of Advisors on Science and Technology that provide advice to the Executive Branch on science and technology policy; and

(B) to the interagency committees and panels of the Federal Government concerned with science and technology.

In carrying out these duties, the statute directs STPI to consult widely with representatives from private industry, academia, and nonprofit institutions, and to incorporate their views in STPI's work to the maximum extent practicable. In addition, the statute requires STPI to submit an annual report to the President on its activities, in accordance with requirements prescribed by the President.

In addition to OSTP and NSF, other STPI sponsors include: the National Institutes of Health, Federal Bureau of Investigation, Department of Energy, and the Department of Commerce.

---

a Full-time employees are defined as those with approximately 80% or more of their work time devoted to STPI work.

b E-mail communication from STPI Deputy Director Bill Brykczynski to CRS, January 11, 2012.

---

[52] In an e-mail from OSTP General Counsel Rachael Leonard on January 24, 2012, OSTP asserted that it may reimburse agencies for all or part of the personnel costs, but is not required to do so under the terms of 3 U.S.C. §112, the provisions of which apply only to the White House Office, the Executive Residence at the White House, the Office of the Vice President, the Domestic Policy Staff, and the Office of Administration.

The Clinton, G.W. Bush, and Obama Administrations have all relied on detailees and fellows to conduct much of OSTP's activities. The OSTP does not include information on detailees and fellows it its budget request to Congress each year, so information regarding their number is irregularly available. Toward the end of the Clinton Administration, OSTP had approximately 60 detailees and fellows. During the G.W. Bush Administration, OSTP had approximately 30-40 detailees per year.[53] Approximately 65 detailees and fellows support the current OSTP.[54] In contrast, 11 detailees worked at OSTP in FY1992.[55]

Figure 2. OSTP Funding, FY1977-FY2012

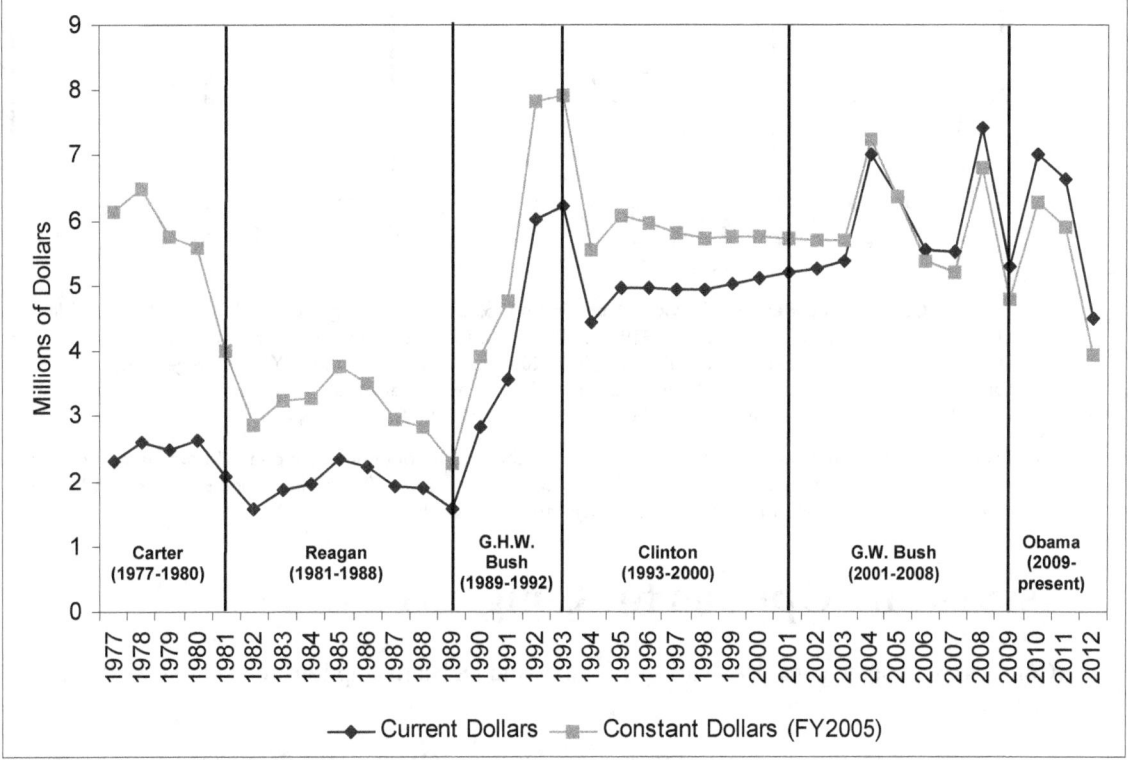

Source: Congressional Research Service. Data from OMB Public Budget Database, congressional appropriation acts, and committee reports, FY1977-FY2012.

Notes: With the exception of FY2008, funding for STPI not included. In FY2008, Congress explicitly appropriated to OSTP $2.240 million for STPI. If the STPI funding is omitted, FY2008 funding for OSTP is $5.184 million in current dollars. The continuing resolution provides FY2013 funding through March 27, 2013, at essentially same rate as in FY2012 rate.

---

[53] Office of Science and Technology Policy, personal communication, August 18, 2008.

[54] Office of Science and Technology Policy, personal communication, January 24, 2012.

[55] U.S. Congress, House Committee on Appropriations, Subcommittee on Departments of Veterans Affairs and Housing and Urban Development, and Independent Agency Appropriations for 1995, *National Science Foundation and Office of Science and Technology Policy*, hearing, 103rd Cong., 2nd sess., 1994.

Figure 3. OSTP Staffing FY1990-FY2010

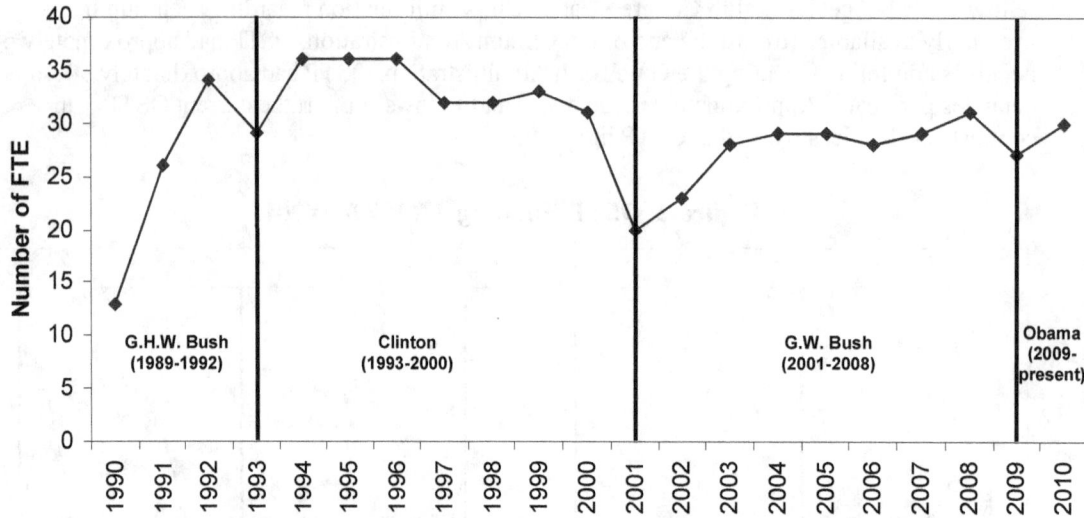

Source: Congressional Research Service. Data is from U.S. Office of Management and Budget, *Budget of the United States Government*, Appendix, FY1979-FY2009. (Note that actual staffing numbers are provided two years later. For example, to determine actual staffing in FY2007, one must review the FY2009 budget request.). The OMB did not provide this data for FY2001. Estimate for this fiscal year based on information provided by OSTP. (E-mail communication between CRS and OSTP on August 18, 2008).

Notes: Data reported is in full-time equivalents (FTE, the amount of effort from one full-time employee over one year) and may not equal number of staff. Data does not include staff or FTEs funded by agencies other than OSTP. Data includes full-time equivalent of holiday and overtime hours.

Issues and Options for Congress

Congress may opt to consider a variety of issues and legislative options related to OSTP. These include:

- the need for science advice within the Executive Office of the President;

- the compliance of OSTP with statutory restrictions on the use of appropriated funds;

- the title, rank, roles, and responsibilities of the OSTP Director;

- the number and policy foci of OSTP Associate Directors;

- the funding and staffing levels provided for OSTP;

- the participation of OSTP and NSTC in federal agency coordination, priority-setting, and budget allocation;

- the role of OSTP in ensuring scientific integrity in federally funded and supported research, including the communication of scientific and technical information by federal agency scientists and engineers; and

- the stature and influence of PCAST.

The following sections address each of these issues, as well as Obama Administration efforts and policy options for Congress.

Need for Science Advice within the Executive Office of the President

One fundamental question is whether the President requires high-level S&T advice, and, if so, whether this advice should take the form of a full-time advisor or presidential advisory committee. Similarly, if the President requires such advice, should part of the EOP, part of a federal department or agency, or an independent agency perform these roles and functions.[56]

Presidents and their senior advisors may believe that they base most of their decisions on factors other than detailed scientific knowledge, such that they perceive a need for only very general S&T knowledge. They may consider opinions from an S&T advisor or a related presidential advisory committee unnecessary and observe no need for such entities to build support for White House decisions. Even when Presidents and their senior advisors rely on high-level S&T advice, certain tensions permeate this process.

A President may believe that high-level S&T advice will do more harm than good if the S&T advisor or presidential advisory committee does not commit to the President's agenda or represent the Administration's perspective. Conversely, the S&T community may fear a close relationship between the S&T advisor and the President will lead to the politicization of S&T advice and subvert the S&T advisor's independence and objectivity. A historical review of presidential S&T activities since the Franklin D. Roosevelt Administration illustrates that differences in opinion between the President and the majority of the S&T community place a presidential S&T advisor or advisory committee in a challenging position. Dismissal or marginalization of S&T consideration from the White House inner circle may result.[57]

On the other hand, an Administration may benefit from an S&T advisor who understands these sensitivities, as the S&T advisor may provide confidential advice privately and speak authoritatively on S&T-related issues for the Administration publicly. The S&T advisor can help assess S&T related departments and agencies, resolve competing claims among these agencies, coordinate the efforts of R&D agencies and the external S&T community in national emergencies, and anticipate new and emerging S&T issues. In addition, presidential advisory committees provide an ongoing ability to engage the S&T community when the President feels the need for external advice.[58]

Consider OSTP Organizational Position

Congress formalized a mechanism for EOP S&T advice when it created OSTP. After assessing the success of OSTP in providing the type of S&T advice envisioned by Congress, Congress may choose to alter the formal mechanisms for EOP S&T advice by changing OSTP's authorization and organizational location.

---

[56] The discussion in this section is based, in part, on Chapter 8, "Science Advisers at the Presidential Level," in Bruce L.R. Smith, *The Advisers: Scientists in the Policy Process* (Washington, DC: The Brookings Institution 1992).

[57] Ibid.

[58] Ibid.

Some in Congress have recommended the elimination of OSTP, characterizing its role as duplicative and ambiguous. Doing so would effectively remove the formal S&T advice mechanism from the EOP. This may lead the EOP to rely on outside groups for S&T advice and lower the overall consideration given to S&T during the policy-making process. In assessing this option, Congress may wish to note that it has eliminated other legislative and executive branch agencies engaged in S&T policy, notably Congress's Office of Technology Assessment in 1995 and the Department of Commerce's Technology Administration and its Office of Technology Policy in 2007. Currently, the Office of Science and Technology Policy is the only federal agency whose principal responsibility is the broad tableau of federal S&T policy. Some S&T policy experts assert that the elimination of S&T policy agencies has made consideration of broader S&T policies more challenging for both the Executive Branch and Congress.

Another alternative is to move OSTP out of the EOP. Once out of the EOP, Congress might establish OSTP as part of an existing department or agency or as a new independent agency. Removing OSTP from the EOP might increase OSTP independence and provide a more optimal distance between the President and the OSTP director. If OSTP became a separate agency, Congress might also benefit from having more control over OSTP's interagency coordination and other activities. If Congress removed OSTP from the EOP, however, policymakers might also view OSTP as sufficiently distant from presidential decisions that neither the Administration nor federal agencies would respond sufficiently to its advice or requests. The S&T community objected when President Nixon moved the precursor to OSTP from the EOP to NSF; they might launch a similar objection now.

Congress might elect to maintain the OSTP function and to keep it within the EOP. If so, Congress may wish to consider OSTP's autonomy. Congressional options regarding OSTP autonomy include whether to continue to provide OSTP with legislative guidance, increase the intensity with which it provides such guidance, or increase presidential authority over OSTP. These options are discussed in more depth below.

Continue Current OSTP Legislative Guidance Mechanisms

Some Members of Congress may believe that no changes need to be made in OSTP operations. Others may believe that taking legislative action regarding OSTP would be neither efficient nor effective given its presence in the EOP and the nature of its activities. As described in this report, OSTP and its affiliated organizations have constantly evolved, responding to the changing needs of the Administration and society, as well as to new scientific and technical challenges and opportunities.

Currently, the President has discretion over the policies, structure, and personnel of OSTP, NSTC, and PCAST. Congress annually oversees OSTP through the regular authorization and appropriation processes and introduces issue-specific bills that identify issues, actions, and functions on which Members of Congress believe OSTP should focus. This approach may be appropriate given the separation of powers between the legislative and executive branches inherent in the U.S. Constitution.

Congress currently holds hearings as part of the presidential appointee confirmation process, part of the appropriation process, and on issues of interest to a given committee. Through the hearing process and other legislative actions, such as introducing bills, passing laws, and writing related report language, Congress provides direction and guidance to OSTP.

One challenge in undertaking these actions is that OSTP might receive overlapping or conflicting guidance. Resolving these conflicts may prove difficult. Additionally, Congress may mandate specific activities or priorities. In such a case, OSTP might need to choose between prioritizing its general statutory roles and responsibilities and specific activities and priorities mandated by Congress.

Similarly, another issue that may arise is when congressional language, either in statute or report, conflicts with presidential activities. For example, a current constitutional issue related to executive branch authority is OSTP's use of appropriated funds for international activities that Congress proscribed. This issue is discussed in detail in the section, "OSTP Compliance with Statutory Restrictions on the Use of Appropriated Funds."

Increase Intensity of OSTP Oversight Mechanisms

Should Congress wish to take a greater role in directing the activities of OSTP, it might consider holding additional specific oversight hearings on OSTP or amending OSTP's organic legislation to reflect current congressional priorities. For example, Congress might legislatively direct OSTP to designate staff or undertake activities focused on an issue of concern. Such legislative language might lead to investment of effort more appropriate to congressional priorities. Establishing such specific priorities and personnel in statute may limit agency discretion, potentially reducing its ability to address other parts of its statutory mission, while securing a focus on specified topics. In addition, this approach may largely consume OSTP staff and budget, inhibiting its ability to respond to new and emerging S&T topics.

Allow President Autonomy over OSTP

Given OSTP's presence within the EOP, Congress might opt to allow the President to manage OSTP as he or she wishes. In this case, Congress would reduce the amount of direction provided to OSTP through oversight hearings, legislation, and report language. The President, with Senate confirmation, would continue to appoint the OSTP Director and Associate Directors; determine OSTP's policy agenda; and organize the management of the office. The President could also continue to use executive orders to manage other activities, such as the formation of NSTC and PCAST.[59]

General Considerations

An important factor for policymakers to consider when weighing these and other options is that personal considerations of the President and the S&T advisor may have a significant effect on the impact of S&T policy advice. These considerations include the strength of the personal relationship of the OSTP director/APST/science advisor, regardless of title, with the President. While one President may decide to rely heavily on the advice of such an advisor, another may decide to rely only minimally upon it due to personal reasons. For example, a President who

---

[59] Note that other organizations besides OSTP, NSTC, and PCAST provide analysis and advice to the White House, Congress, and federal agencies. For example, Congress often asks that the National Academy of Sciences or the National Science Board provide this guidance. for further information, see, for example, Roger Pielke, Jr., "Who Has the Ear of the President?," *Nature*, 450:347-348, November 15, 2007, http://sciencepolicy.colorado.edu/admin/publication_files/resource-2574-2007.28.pdf.

believes that the primary role of an S&T advisor is to support and express the views of the Administration might be less likely to rely on an S&T advisor invested in providing independent advice and judgment. Similarly, if the President or other top EOP officials generally are interested in S&T policy or strongly believe S&T advice should factor importantly in their decision making, they may solicit S&T policy advice. Officials who do not consider S&T important factors may not solicit input from an S&T advisor, regardless of title or position.

OSTP Compliance with Statutory Restrictions on the Use of Appropriated Funds

Congress has sought to restrict OSTP from engaging in certain activities by prohibiting the use of appropriated funds for these activities. The current continuing resolution, the FY2012 and the FY2011 appropriations bills all included such restrictions. Specifically, Section 1340(a) of the Department of Defense and Full-Year Continuing Appropriations Act, 2011 (P.L. 112-10) prohibited OSTP from expending funds made available under Division B of the act

> to develop, design, plan, promulgate, implement, or execute a bilateral policy, program, order, or contract of any kind to participate, collaborate, or coordinate bilaterally in any way with China or any Chinese-owned company unless such activities are specifically authorized by a law enacted after the date of enactment of this division.[60]

The Department of Justice (DOJ) and OSTP have asserted that the President's constitutional authority to conduct foreign diplomacy precludes Congress from proscribing the use of funds for such specific activities. The OSTP expended a portion of its FY2011 appropriation to engage in activities with China that Section 1340(a) sought to proscribe. The OSTP has asserted that "certain applications of Section 1340 ... would infringe upon the President's constitutional authority to conduct foreign diplomacy."[61] Subsequently, DOJ issued a supporting opinion on the constitutionality of the application of Section 1340 to OSTP's activities concluding, in part:

> Section 1340(a) of the Department of Defense and Full-Year Continuing Appropriations Act, 2011 is unconstitutional as applied to certain activities undertaken pursuant to the President's constitutional authority to conduct the foreign relations of the United States.

> Most, if not all, of the activities of the Office of Science and Technology Policy that we have been asked to consider fall within the President's exclusive power to conduct diplomacy, and OSTP's officers and employees therefore may engage in those activities as agents designated by the President for the conduct of diplomacy, notwithstanding Section 1340(a).[62]

In contrast, the Government Accountability Office (GAO), in response to a request from House Commerce, Justice, Science, and Related Agencies Subcommittee Chairman Wolf, concluded that

---

[60] §1340(a), Division B, P.L. 112-10.

[61] Response of John Holdren, Director, OSTP, *Questions for the Record, Office of Science and Technology Policy,* Hearing on May 4, 2011, available in *Commerce, Justice, Science, and Related Agencies Appropriations for 2012,* committee print, prepared by U.S. Government Printing Office, 112th Cong., 1st sess., May 4, 2011 (Washington: GPO, 2011), pp. 316-328.

[62] U.S. Department of Justice, *Unconstitutional Restrictions on Activities of the Office of Science And Technology Policy in Section 1340(A) of The Department Of Defense And Full-Year Continuing Appropriations Act, 2011,* Memorandum Opinion for the General Counsel, Office of Science and Technology Policy, Washington, DC, September 19, 2011, http://www.justice.gov/olc/2011/conduct-diplomacy.pdf.

... OSTP's use of appropriations to fund its participation in the [U.S.-China Dialogue on Innovation Policy] and [U.S.-China Strategic and Economic Dialogue] violated the prohibition in Section 1340. In addition, because Section 1340 prohibited the use of OSTP's appropriations for this purpose, OSTP's involvement in the Innovation Dialogue and the S&ED resulted in obligations in excess of appropriated funds available to OSTP; as such, OSTP violated the Antideficiency Act, 31 U.S.C. §1341(a)(1)(A).[63]

With respect to the issue of the constitutionality of the law, GAO stated:

It is not our role nor within our province to opine or adjudicate the constitutionality of duly enacted statutes such as Section 1340. In our view, legislation that was passed by Congress and signed by the President, thereby satisfying the Constitution's bicameralism and presentment requirements, is entitled to a heavy presumption in favor of constitutionality.[64]

Citing the GAO conclusion, Chairman Wolf asked Attorney General Eric Holder to convey his expectation that the Attorney General "will ensure comprehensive enforcement of Section 1340(a)" of P.L. 112-10 and "hold [OSTP Director] Dr. Holdren to full account for violation of the Anti-Deficiency Act."[65]

Congress subsequently reduced OSTP's FY2012 appropriations by nearly a third (32.3%). The House Committee on Appropriations had sought to reduce OSTP funding by half. Further, statutory language in OSTP's FY2012 appropriations act (P.L. 112-55)[66] and language in the accompanying report (H.Rept. 112-284) prohibit OSTP from using appropriated funds to support activities that would carry the risk of transferring sensitive technology to China. In contrast with the FY2011 language, Section 539 of the law allows OSTP to proceed with activities that it certifies pose no risk of transfer.[67]

The Continuing Appropriations Resolution, 2013 (P.L. 112-175) extends the statutory language found in P.L. 112-55 through March 27, 2013. It also provides funding for OSTP at the FY2012 rate increased by 0.612% through March 27, 2013.

Congress might continue to assert its authority to restrict OSTP activities. Congress might continue to include language restricting or prohibiting OSTP from using appropriations, might reduce OSTP's annual appropriations to encourage compliance with statutory language, and might amend OSTP's organic statute with restrictive provisions. Alternatively, Congress may opt to acknowledge that the President's authority to designate agents (i.e., OSTP) to serve on his behalf in the conduct of diplomacy might permit some OSTP activities proscribed by current law. Finally, Congress could opt to remove existing restrictions entirely or to not include such restrictions in future appropriations laws.

---

[63] U.S. Government Accountability Office, *Office of Science and Technology Policy—Bilateral Activities with China*, B-321982, October 11, 2011, p. 1.

[64] Ibid., p. 4.

[65] Letter from Rep. Frank R. Wolf, Chairman, Subcommittee on Commerce, Justice, Science, and Related Agencies, Committee on Appropriations, to The Hon. Eric H. Holder, Jr., Attorney General, U.S. Department of Justice, October 13, 2011.

[66] Division B, Title V, §539, P.L. 112-55

[67] Such certification must be submitted to the House and Senate Committees at least 14 days prior to the activity in question.

Title, Rank, Roles, and Responsibilities

Under President Obama, John Holdren serves as both OSTP Director and APST. In contrast, under George W. Bush, John Marburger was given only the title of OSTP Director.[68] Some experts in the S&T community have proposed that the OSTP Director also be given the title of APST or cabinet rank.[69] A related issue is whether or not the roles and responsibilities of the OSTP Director should be undertaken by several appointees rather than one. To a large extent, the appointment of an advisor to a particular position or title arises from presidential discretion. Consequently, this presidential discretion may limit the ability of Congress to require greater or lesser degrees of access to the President and other key administration decision makers.

Title and Rank

As shown in the **Appendix**, presidential science advisors have held a variety of titles since the Franklin D. Roosevelt Administration. Of the 12 Administrations reviewed, the most common title has been some variation of Science Advisor to the President (five Administrations), followed by Special Assistant to the President (four Administrations). The OSTP Director held the title of APST in the George H.W. Bush and Clinton Administrations but not in the George W. Bush Administration. President Obama appointed John Holdren as APST and OSTP Director; the Senate subsequently confirmed Dr. Holdren's nomination as OSTP Director.[70]

The difference between an individual being the OSTP Director and the APST is more than semantic. This section outlines some of the policy issues related to the OSTP Director holding the position of APST or being given cabinet rank.

Congressional Testimony

Some Members of Congress may wish to oversee who is appointed as the president's science advisor and to have the option of hearing testimony from the individual serving in that role.

---

[68] At no time have the positions of OSTP Director and APST been filled by different people.

[69] See for example, Carnegie Commission on Science, Technology, and Government, *Science & Technology and the President* (New York: Carnegie Corporation of New York, October 1988), http://www.carnegie.org/sub/pubs/ science_tech/nextadm.htm; Henry Kelly, Ivan Oelrich, Steven Aftergood, and Benn H. Tannenbaum, *Flying Blind: The Rise, Fall and Possible Resurrection of Science Policy Advice in the United States* (Washington, DC: Federation of American Scientists, 2004), http://www.fas.org/pubs/_docs/flying_blind.pdf; Ensuring the Best Presidential Appointments in the New Administration, Committee on Science, Engineering, and Public Policy, *Science and Technology for America's Progress: Ensuring the Best Presidential Appointments in the New Administration* (Washington, DC: National Academy Press, 2008), http://www.nap.edu/catalog.php?record_id=12481; Jennifer Sue Bond, Mark Schaefer, David Rejeski, Rodney W. Nichols, *OSTP 2.0: Critical Upgrade: Enhancing Capacity for White House Science and Technology Policymaking: Recommendations for the Next President* (Washington, DC: Woodrow Wilson International Center for Scholars, June 2008), http://wilsoncenter.org/news/docs/OSTP%20Paper1.pdf; and Center for the Study of the Presidency, Study Group on Presidential Science and Technology Personnel Advisory Assets, "Presidential Leadership to Ensure Science and Technology in Service of National Needs: A Report to the 2008 Candidates," http://www.thepresidency.org/pubs/science_tech_2008.pdf.

[70] Executive Order 13539 signed by President Obama specifically designates that the Assistant to the President for Science and Technology shall serve as a co-chair of PCAST, along with one or two of the non-federal members of PCAST. Executive Order 13226, signed by President George W. Bush, stated that the President would designate a "Federal Government official" to serve as a member and co-chair of PCAST. President Bush's designated co-chair was John Marburger, who was his OSTP Director.

Others may not place great emphasis on overseeing the role of OSTP Director or APST and may have other sources from which they can obtain S&T analysis and information.

Congress expects that an executive branch official who administers a department or agency established by law will testify before it. This contrasts with an individual whose sole responsibility is to advise the President. Some presidential advisors, such as the Director of OSTP, are in units of the EOP established by law and are also subject to confirmation by the Senate. Accordingly, Congress often asks OSTP Directors to testify before it,[71] and may, if necessary, compel them to do so. However, an APST may assert the right to not testify before Congress in accordance with the principles of separation of powers and/or executive privilege.[72] Some members of the S&T community contend that Congress should permit an individual serving as APST to discriminate between privileged advice to the President that should not be disclosed to Congress and information appropriate to disclose to Congress.[73] If Congress desires to ensure the availability of the APST for testimony, it might opt to establish the position of APST by statute and require Senate confirmation. Some experts have expressed concern regarding confusion that might arise if Congress could require some Administration staff with "Assistant to the President" titles to testify, but not others.[74] Others have asserted that this might not be an effective approach since, even if such a position were established by statute, a President might opt not to nominate someone for that position or possibly even appoint someone to a similarly titled position that does not exist in statute.

Cabinet Rank

Some members of the S&T community have expressed their desire for the OSTP Director to have a greater role and influence in the development of Administration policy. They assert that statutorily designating the OSTP Director as a cabinet-level position would provide such an enhanced role and influence. In their view, the President would identify an individual nominated for the cabinet-level OSTP Director position at the same time as other cabinet members, shortly after the election of a new Administration. If also appointed to serve as APST, the individual could begin work immediately, though exercise of the duties of OSTP Director, with its enhanced stature, would have to await formal nomination and Senate confirmation.[75] If appointed early in a new Administration, some experts in the S&T community contend, the individual filling the

---

[71] For example, Obama Administration OSTP Director Holdren has testified on international science and technology cooperation; federal R&D funding; climate change; STEM education; the future of U.S. human space flight; and innovation and competitiveness. Bush Administration OSTP Director Marburger testified on similar topics, as well as concerns about political interference with research; information technology R&D program oversight; windstorm impact reduction; women in academic science and engineering; coal gasification; patents developed with federal research funding; and weather satellites.

[72] Louis Fisher, "White House Aides Testifying before Congress," *Presidential Studies Quarterly*, vol. 27, Winter 1997, p. 140-141. For further discussion, see CRS Report RL31351, *Presidential Advisers' Testimony Before Congressional Committees: An Overview*, by Todd Garvey, Alissa M. Dolan, and Henry B. Hogue.

[73] See, for example, Henry Kelly, Ivan Oelrich, Steven Aftergood, and Benn H. Tannenbaum, *Flying Blind: The Rise, Fall and Possible Resurrection of Science Policy Advice in the United States* (Washington, DC: Federation of American Scientists, 2004), http://www.fas.org/pubs/_docs/flying_blind.pdf.

[74] In an e-mail from OSTP General Counsel Rachael Leonard on January 24, 2012, OSTP stated that "As OSTP Director, Dr. Holdren signed a statement to the Senate Commerce committee prior to his confirmation hearing that he would be available to testify. No OSTP APST or OSTP Director/APST has declined to testify."

[75] National Academies, Committee on Science, Engineering, and Public Policy, *Science and Technology for America's Progress: Ensuring the Best Presidential Appointments in a New Administration* (Washington, DC: National Academy Press, 2008), http://www.nap.edu/catalog.php?record_id=12481.

APST position could help identify and recruit the best scientists, engineers, and health professionals for the approximately 100 S&T policy-related presidential appointments.[76]

Additionally, some contend that an APST/OSTP Director with cabinet rank would have greater access to the President and other senior Administration staff.[77] They assert that cabinet rank status would enhance the OSTP Director's authority and influence in incorporating scientific and technical viewpoints into Administration decision-making. Others contend that the issue of cabinet-rank for the APST/OSTP Director status is trivial and would be unlikely to substantially improve the APST/OSTP Director's role and influence in EOP activities, including Cabinet meetings.[78]

From a historical perspective, some experts believe that Presidents and their science advisors have unique and idiosyncratic relationships. To these experts, a more important question is how an administration manages and uses the infrastructure of expert advice it inherits.[79] Another perspective is that the organization of the White House determines the S&T advisor's status and access. According to this perspective, if the President relies primarily on a group of White House staff members for advice, the advisor should be the APST. If the Cabinet is the primary source of advice, than the science advisor should be made a member of the Cabinet. From this perspective, the title itself is less important than the access to the President that it provides.[80] Other critics contend that rather than focusing on the title, the S&T community should instead focus on the degree to which a presidential administration is transparent about its operations.[81]

Roles and Responsibilities

As discussed earlier, historically OSTP Directors advise the President on S&T policy formulation, R&D budget issues, the policy significance of scientific and technical developments, and STEM education, among other things.[82] In addition, when holding the APST title, the OSTP Director

---

[76] For a list of the 50 to 60 S&T policy appointments deemed most urgent by the National Academies, see National Academies, Committee on Science, Engineering, and Public Policy, *Science and Technology for America's Progress: Ensuring the Best Presidential Appointments in a New Administration* (Washington, DC: National Academy Press, 2008), http://www.nap.edu/catalog.php?record_id=12481.

[77] National Academies, Committee on Science, Engineering, and Public Policy, *Science and Technology for America's Progress: Ensuring the Best Presidential Appointments in a New Administration* (Washington, DC: National Academy Press, 2008), http://www.nap.edu/catalog.php?record_id=12481.

[78] Based on CRS discussions with Stanley Sokul, Bush Administration Chief of Staff, OSTP, August 14, 2008.

[79] Roger Pielke, Jr., "Who Has the Ear of the President?," *Nature* 450:347-348, November 15, 2007, http://www.nature.com/nature/journal/v450/n7168/full/450347a.html.

[80] National Academies, *Science and Technology Advice in the White House: Recommendations for President-Elect George Bush* (Washington, DC: National Academy Press, 1988)

[81] For a discussion of this issue, see David Goldston, "US Election: Not the Best Advice." *Nature*, 455:453, September 24, 2008, http://www.nature.com/news/2008/080924/full/455453a.html.

[82] Based on Carnegie Commission on Science, Technology, and Government, *Science & Technology and the President* (New York: Carnegie Corporation of New York, October 1988); National Academies, *Science and Technology Advice in the White House: Recommendations for President-Elect George Bush* (Washington, DC: National Academy Press, 1988); and National Academies, Committee on Science, Engineering, and Public Policy, *Science and Technology for America's Progress: Ensuring the Best Presidential Appointments in the New Administration* (Washington, DC: National Academy Press, 2008), http://www.nap.edu/catalog.php?record_id=12481.

---

manages the NSTC and co-chairs PCAST.[83] In addition, OSTP Directors can serve as a communication conduit between the EOP and the federal and non-federal S&T community.

The Obama Administration has opted to consolidate all of these functions under a single individual, John Holdren, who has the dual roles of OSTP Director and APST. President Obama has appointed four Associate Directors with responsibility for discrete policy areas: science, technology, environment and energy, and national security and international affairs. Under the Obama Administration, the OSTP Director:

- Works with OMB in the development of the President's R&D budget request.

- Provides advice to the President and senior Administration officials on policies for science and technology (including R&D and STEM education).

- Provides advice to the President and senior Administration officials on the application of science and technology in support of a wide range of national policies (e.g., economic, military, space, health, environmental, agricultural policies).

- Represents the United States in international S&T policy related meetings.

- Manages the NSTC and co-chairs PCAST in his capacity as APST.

- Is responsible for performing functions related to disaster communications as assigned in Executive Order 12472, Assignment of National Security and Emergency Preparedness Telecommunications Functions.

One alternative for Congress is to change the current statutory structure and duties of OSTP, separating the various OSTP roles and responsibilities and establishing separate positions and/or organizations for each. For example, the S&T community has debated the utility of having two different individuals serve as APST and OSTP Director. While some believe having two people serve in these roles might enhance the ability and potential of an APST to be part of the President's inner circle, others believe the potential for conflict between the two is high.[84] Similarly, some members of the S&T community have suggested that the President appoint co-equal officials, one responsible for science policy and the other for technology policy. Shortly after assuming office, President Obama created the new title of Chief Technology Officer within the EOP, but assigned it to his choice for Associate Director of OSTP for Technology.[85] While signaling that this appointee is the Administration's point person for technology issues, the individual holding the title is in a position subordinate to the OSTP Director.[86] Some S&T policy experts have expressed concerns that bifurcation of authorities and responsibilities might create conflicts and a lack of integration. [87]

---

[83] In practice, President George W. Bush's OSTP Director managed the NSTC and co-chaired PCAST even in the absence of a joint appointment as APST.

[84] National Academies, Committee on Science, Engineering, and Public Policy, *Science and Technology in the National Interest: Ensuring the Best Presidential and Federal Advisory Committee Science and Technology Appointments* (Washington, DC: National Academy Press, 2005), http://www.nap.edu/catalog.php?record_id=11152.

[85] Aneesh Chopra was the first Chief Technology Officer. Todd Park succeeded him in 2012.

[86] For more information on the possible chief technology officer position, see CRS Report R40150, *A Federal Chief Technology Officer in the Obama Administration: Options and Issues for Consideration*, by John F. Sargent Jr.

[87] David Hatch, "Tech Czar Might Rule Policy under Obama," *Congressional Daily*, September 10, 2008, http://www.nationaljournal.com/congressdaily/cda_20080910_6421.php?related=true&story1=cda_20080910_6421& (continued...)

Another challenge in splitting the functions of OSTP and assigning them to separate individuals or organizations is the size of OSTP's budget and staff.[88] For example, current resources may not effectively support two senior officials and their associated staffs. Congress might opt to increase funding and authorized staffing levels to support such a reorganization.

Number and Policy Foci of OSTP Associate Directors

Current statutory authority provides flexibility to the President with respect to the number of OSTP Associate Directors (up to four) and the scope of their areas of responsibility (entirely at the discretion of the President).[89] Under President George W. Bush there were two: an Associate Director for Science and an Associate Director for Technology. President Obama has appointed four Associate Directors with responsibility for discrete policy areas: Science, Technology, Environment and Energy, and National Security and International Affairs.

Congress could opt to specify a fixed number of Associate Directors, and could assign some or all of them with specific policy foci. Some Members of Congress have undertaken efforts in this regard. For example, in its report (S.Rept. 110-124) on the Departments of Commerce and Justice, Science, and Related Agencies Appropriations Act, 2008 (S. 1745, 110th Congress), the Senate Committee on Appropriations recommended OSTP create an Associate Director for Earth Science and Application position to coordinate all federal efforts to better understand and predict changes in the earth's climate and oceans.[90] Another bill (H.R. 5116, 111th Congress) would have required the OSTP Director to appoint an Associate Director to serve as the Coordinator for Societal Dimensions of Nanotechnology.

In addition, some members of the S&T community have proposed that one or more of the OSTP Associate Director positions share appointments with the National Economic Council (NEC), National Security Council (NSC), Domestic Policy Council (DPC), and Office of Management and Budget. In this vein, President Obama appointed the OSTP Director and the CTO to the DPC;[91] made Dr. Holdren a member of the NEC by providing him with the APST title;[92] added the Chief Technology Officer (who currently also holds the position of OSTP Associate Director for Technology) as a member of the NEC; and issued Presidential Policy Directive 1 (PPD-1) stating that "When science and technology related issues are on the agenda, the NSC's regular attendees will include the Director of the Office of Science and Technology Policy."[93] Shortly after his appointment Dr. Holdren stated that he expected that the OSTP associate director for

---

(...continued)

story2=cd_20080912_9947&story3=null.

[88] For more information, see "OSTP Budget and Staffing."

[89] 42 U.S.C. §6612.

[90] CRS Report RL34092, *Commerce, Justice, Science, and Related Agencies: FY2008 Appropriations*, coordinated by William J. Krouse.

[91] White House, *Further Amendments to Executive Order 12859, Establishment Of The Domestic Policy Council*, February 5, 2009. For more information, see http://www.whitehouse.gov/the_press_office/Executive-OrderFurther-Amendments-To-Executive-Order-12859Establishment-Of-The-Domestic-Policy-Council/.

[92] White House, *Further Amendments to Executive Order 12835, Establishment of the National Economic Council*, February 5, 2009. For more information, see http://www.whitehouse.gov/the_press_office/Executive-Order-Further-Amendments-to-Executive-Order-12835-Establishment-of-the-National-Economic-Council/

[93] Ibid.

national security would "be dual-hatted" in the National Security Council.[94] According to OSTP, the Associate Director for National Security and International Affairs "necessarily works in close collaboration with the National Security Staff on a wide variety of issues, though the position has not been officially 'dual–hatted' during the Obama Administration."[95]

OSTP Budget and Staffing

The ability of OSTP to perform its statutory duties depends, in part, on the size of its budget and staff. **Figure 2** and **Figure 3**, presented earlier, illustrate OSTP's historical budget and staffing. Between FY1996 and FY2012, the budgets of Presidents Clinton, Bush, and Obama included requests for the authorization of 35-40 full-time equivalent (FTE) positions while the actual number of OSTP-funded staff ranged from 23 to 31. The OSTP has used detailees and fellows to supplement its core staffing. During the George W. Bush Administration, detailees and fellows provided approximately half of OSTP's total staff; during the Clinton Administration, as many as 61 detailees and fellows accounted for approximately two-thirds of total OSTP staff.

Some reports developed by the S&T community express concerns that OSTP needs to have more career civil service professional staff and a larger budget.[96] In their view, additional career staff, which would continue to serve from one presidential administration to the next, would help maintain institutional knowledge and provide a solid understanding of government operations. Such staff might enable a new administration to move more quickly on S&T policy issues and provide enhanced support to political appointees. These reports assert that this change would make OSTP staff similar to other EOP expert staff, such as those employed at OMB.[97]

Additional funding, these reports assert, would also provide OSTP with sufficient staff to conduct special analyses on emerging issues. Currently, such analyses are generally provided by OSTP's federally funded research and development center (FFRDC), the Science and Technology Policy Institute (STPI). (See "Science and Technology Policy Institute" box for more information.)

Congress may wish to maintain the current staffing approach, or it might wish to increase the number of OSTP civil service staff; specify the number of Associate Directors; designate the policy issue focus of the Associate Directors; or authorize or require OSTP, through its Director or Associate Directors, to play a greater role in the activities of other EOP agencies, such as OMB, NEC, DPC, NSC, and CEQ.

Should Congress wish to enhance the funding and staffing of OSTP, it can do so through the appropriations process. Congress provided $6.6 million for OSTP in FY2011, but cut OSTP funding to $4.5 million in FY2012 amid concerns over OSTP's use of funds for activities

---

[94] Jeffrey Mervis, "John Holdren Brings More than Energy to His Role as Science Adviser," *Science*, vol. 324 (April 17, 2009), pp. 324-325.

[95] E-mail communication from OSTP General Counsel Rachael Leonard to CRS, January 24, 2012.

[96] Henry Kelly, Ivan Oelrich, Steven Aftergood, and Benn H. Tannenbaum, *Flying Blind: The Rise, Fall and Possible Resurrection of Science Policy Advice in the United States* (Washington, DC: Federation of American Scientists, 2004), http://www.fas.org/pubs/_docs/flying_blind.pdf; and Jennifer Sue Bond, Mark Schaefer, David Rejeski, Rodney W. Nichols, *OSTP 2.0: Critical Upgrade: Enhancing Capacity for White House Science and Technology Policymaking: Recommendations for the Next President* (Washington, DC: Woodrow Wilson International Center for Scholars, June 2008), http://wilsoncenter.org/news/docs/OSTP%20Paper1.pdf.

[97] According to the FY2009 budget request, OMB's budget is $78 million, which supports 489 staff members. For more information, see http://www.whitehouse.gov/omb/budget/fy2009/pdf/appendix/eop.pdf.

---

proscribed in report language accompanying its FY2011 appropriations (see "OSTP Compliance with Statutory Restrictions on the Use of Appropriated Funds"). The continuing resolution provides effectively FY2012 funding to OSTP through March 27, 2013.

OSTP and NSTC Participation in Federal Agency Coordination, Priority-Setting, and Budget Allocation

As discussed earlier, OSTP, the OSTP Director and Associate Directors, and the NSTC participate in coordinating, setting priorities for, and allocating the budget for federal S&T activities. S&T policy organizations have suggested enhancing this participation.

Role of OSTP Director

Some reports from the S&T community suggest the OSTP Director should take a greater role in coordination, priority-setting, and budget allocation regarding the federal R&D budget;[98] energy;[99] STEM education;[100] international S&T policy;[101] and federal-state S&T policy.[102] In addition, some members of the S&T policy community have suggested that the OSTP Director play a greater role in EOP policy bodies involved in priority-setting and budget allocation, such as the OMB, NEC, CEQ, DPC, and NSC.[103] For example, Congress could require the OSTP Director to play a greater role (e.g., certification of priorities or budgets) in setting priorities at the federal agencies, particularly for multi-agency and inter-agency activities.

Role of NSTC

Another recommendation found in these S&T community reports is to make the NSTC's authority equivalent to that of the NSC.[104] The NSTC, they assert, lacks the influence of NSC.

---

[98] Henry Kelly, Ivan Oelrich, Steven Aftergood, and Benn H. Tannenbaum, *Flying Blind: The Rise, Fall and Possible Resurrection of Science Policy Advice in the United States* (Washington, DC: Federation of American Scientists, 2004), http://www.fas.org/pubs/_docs/flying_blind.pdf.

[99] Senator Jeff Bingaman, "The Energy Challenge We Face and The Strategies We Need," The Karl Taylor Compton Lecture, Massachusetts Institute of Technology, April 25, 2008, http://energy.senate.gov/public/_files/ComptonLectureJFB.pdf.

[100] National Science Board, *National Action Plan for Addressing the Critical Needs of the U.S. Science, Technology, and Mathematics Education System* (Ballston, VA: National Science Foundation, 2007), http://www.nsf.gov/nsb/documents/2007/stem_action.pdf.

[101] National Science Board, *International Science and Engineering Partnerships: A Priority for U.S. Foreign Policy and Our Nation's Innovation Enterprise*, NSB 08-4 (Arlington, VA: National Science Foundation, 2008), http://www.nsf.gov/nsb/publications/2008/nsb084.pdf. Jennifer Sue Bond, Mark Schaefer, David Rejeski, Rodney W. Nichols, *OSTP 2.0: Critical Upgrade: Enhancing Capacity for White House Science and Technology Policymaking: Recommendations for the Next President* (Washington, DC: Woodrow Wilson International Center for Scholars, June 2008), http://wilsoncenter.org/news/docs/OSTP%20Paper1.pdf.

[102] Jennifer Sue Bond, Mark Schaefer, David Rejeski, Rodney W. Nichols, *OSTP 2.0: Critical Upgrade: Enhancing Capacity for White House Science and Technology Policymaking: Recommendations for the Next President* (Washington, DC: Woodrow Wilson International Center for Scholars, June 2008), http://wilsoncenter.org/news/docs/OSTP%20Paper1.pdf.

[103] Ibid.

[104] Henry Kelly, Ivan Oelrich, Steven Aftergood, and Benn H. Tannenbaum, *Flying Blind: The Rise, Fall and Possible Resurrection of Science Policy Advice in the United States* (Washington, DC: Federation of American Scientists, 2004) at http://www.fas.org/pubs/_docs/flying_blind.pdf.

The differences in statutory authority, staff, and budget are among the reasons cited for this disparity.

The NSTC has participated in presidential decision-making processes, but in different manners across administrations. For example, during the Clinton Administration, the NSTC issued six Presidential Review Directives (PRDs). The PRDs served as the basis for gathering information, and policy options for the President. President Clinton then had this information available as he developed eight Presidential Decision Directives (PDD) establishing new policy.[105] As during the G.W. Bush Administration,[106] the NSTC has developed no PRDs or their equivalents during the Obama Administration.

Some experts in the S&T community believe incorporating NSTC deliberations into policy documents rather than basing the policy documents on formal directives puts S&T and the NSTC in a supportive role, regardless of the issue. These experts assert that S&T input and ramifications should exert a more prominent influence on public policy in some situations.[107]

During his Senate confirmation hearing, Holdren discussed his vision for the NSTC:

> There is an entity called the National Science and Technology Council which has existed in the White House, organized by the Office of Science and Technology Policy, but bringing together all of the executive branch agencies, typically at the deputy level, that have roles in science and technology.
>
> This is a place where in the past one has been able to address crosscutting and overlapping jurisdiction issues effectively. In the last 8 years, it has languished. It was not really fully utilized in the last administration, but our intention—certainly my intention, if confirmed—would be to revive it and utilize it fully to try to reduce the sorts of problems that you point to here.[108]

In this regard, the Obama Administration asserts that it has undertaken efforts to revitalize and streamline the efforts of the NSTC. In this regard, the Administration cites its establishment of a fifth NSTC committee—the Committee on Science, Technology, Engineering, and Math (STEM) Education—to coordinate Federal programs and activities in support of STEM education. The Administration states that under President Obama NSTC committees meet two or three times annually and each subcommittee meets at least quarterly. The Administration also asserts that it "oversaw the restructuring of the original NSTC committees, with elimination of interagency efforts, where appropriate, and initiation of new efforts, as indicated by Administration priorities and/or Congressional mandates."[109]

---

[105] A list is available at http://www.fas.org/irp/offdocs/direct.htm.

[106] Based on CRS discussions with Stanley Sokul, Bush Administration Chief of Staff, OSTP, August 25, 2008.

[107] Henry Kelly, Ivan Oelrich, Steven Aftergood, and Benn H. Tannenbaum, *Flying Blind: The Rise, Fall and Possible Resurrection of Science Policy Advice in the United States* (Washington, DC: Federation of American Scientists, 2004) at http://www.fas.org/pubs/_docs/flying_blind.pdf.

[108] U.S. Congress, Senate Committee on Commerce, Science, and Transportation, *Nominations to the Executive Office of the President and the Department of Commerce*, committee print, prepared by U.S. Government Printing Office, 110th Cong., 1st sess., February 12, 2009, S. Hrg. 111-408 (Washington: GPO, 2009), pp. 51-471.

[109] E-mail communication from OSTP General Counsel Rachael Leonard to CRS, January 24, 2012.

Options for Congress

Congress might choose to leave the roles of the OSTP Director and the NSTC in the budget process unchanged, might choose to increase their authorities, or might choose to increase oversight of their roles.

Congress might mandate that OSTP review agency S&T budgets prior to submission to OMB and empower OSTP to alter the distribution of funding between S&T priorities based on their relative importance. Such authority might increase the ability of OSTP to harmonize and coordinate S&T expenditures among federal agencies. Federal agencies might resist such a change in authority, as it might further complicate the budget development and submission process and create competition between OSTP and OMB directives.

Congress might require that NSTC or OSTP review agency S&T budgets to identify correspondence between NSTC multi-agency R&D strategies and federal investments. A hallmark of multi-agency R&D investment is the need to coordinate the magnitude and mission goals of agency investments in order to achieve broader federal R&D goals. Such a review might increase transparency regarding progress towards these broader federal R&D goals, but might also require increases in available resources. Identifying cross-cutting funding and efforts may require dedicated program offices and staff to track and report on multi-agency activities.

Congress might choose to formalize the NSTC structure and organization and provide additional funding and personnel to increase the robustness of its process. Providing statutory underpinnings to the NSTC may enable Congress to obtain greater insight into the activities of the NSTC through reporting requirements and oversight of its activities. Alternatively, Congress could mandate that the OSTP Director provide regular reports on the activities of the NSTC.

OSTP Role in Ensuring Scientific Integrity

The OSTP plays a role in ensuring the scientific integrity of research conducted and supported by the federal government, as well as in the communication of scientific and technical information developed and analyzed by federal scientists and engineers. For example, OSTP, as part of a process managed by OMB, reviews S&T-related testimony to Congress.[110]

George W. Bush Administration

During the George W. Bush Administration, advocacy groups charged that politicization adversely affected the integrity of science, primarily that related to environment, public health, and national security issues.[111] These groups contended that Administration officials restricted the ability of federal scientists and engineers to provide information, instructed them to change their

---

[110] The review process is governed by OMB Circular No. A-19.

[111] See, for example, Union of Concerned Scientists, *Scientific Integrity in Policymaking: An Investigation into the Bush Administration's Misuse of Science*, March 2004, http://www.ucsusa.org/assets/documents/scientific_integrity/ rsi_final_fullreport_1.pdf; Union of Concerned Scientists, *Federal Science and the Public Good: Securing the Integrity of Science in Policy Making*, February 2008, http://ucsusa.org/scientific_integrity/solutions/big_picture_solutions/ federal-science-and-the.html; and Rena Steinzor, Wendy Wagner, and Matthew Shudtz, *Saving Science from Politics: Nine Essential Reforms of the Legal System*, Center for Progressive Reform, July 2008, http://www.progressivereform.org/articles/SavingScience805.pdf.

research reports, or modified the congressional testimony of federal scientific and technical agency leadership that did not support the Administration's views. OSTP Director Marburger stated that such allegations were "sweeping generalizations based on a patchwork of disjointed facts and accusations that reach conclusions that are wrong and misleading."[112]

Policymakers responded to these concerns in several ways. In the America COMPETES Act (P.L. 110-69, §1009), Congress directed OSTP to develop an overarching set of principles to ensure the communication and open exchange of data by federal scientists and engineers. On May 28, 2008, in response to this requirement, OSTP sent a memorandum to federal agencies that sponsor research. The memorandum provides guidance and what OSTP termed the "Core Principle for Communication of the Results of Scientific Research Conducted by Scientists Employed by Federal Civilian Agencies." It states:

> Robust and open communication of scientific information is critical not only for advancing science, but also for ensuring that society is informed and provided with objective and factual information to make sound decisions. Accordingly, the Federal government is committed to a culture of scientific openness that fosters and protects the open exchange of ideas, data and information to the scientific community, policymakers, and the public.[113]

The memorandum also indicated that NASA's science communications policy should be a model for other federal agencies:[114] NASA policy states that, "In keeping with the desire for a culture of openness, NASA employees may, consistent with this policy, speak to the press and the public about their work," with exceptions for privileged and other controlled information.[115]

Science and Technology Policy Groups

Prior to President Obama's inauguration, some S&T policy advocacy groups proposed that the Executive Branch change its scientific communication policy.[116] One proposal was for the issuance of an executive order requiring federal agency leadership to monitor scientific integrity within their agencies and submit an annual report to OSTP with their observations and actions.

Other proposals included: reversing Executive Order 13422 to prevent OMB from conducting political reviews of scientific documents;[117] enhancing whistleblower protections, including

---

[112] See, for example, OSTP, "Statement by President Bush's Science Adviser and Director of the Office of Science and Technology Policy John H. Marburger III on Union of Concerned Scientists Document and Press Release," press release, http://www.ostp.gov/galleries/press_release_files/jhmStatementUCS27-8-04.pdf.

[113] OSTP, "Principles for the Release of Scientific Research Results," Memorandum, May 28, 2008, http://www.ostp.gov/galleries/default-file/Research%20Results.pdf. Note that this memorandum regards the communication of scientific data and information, not science and technology policy.

[114] NASA's policy is available at http://www.nasa.gov/pdf/145687main_information_policy.pdf.

[115] 14 C.F.R. 1213.102.

[116] Union of Concerned Scientists, *Federal Science and the Public Good: Securing the Integrity of Science in Policy Making*, February 2008, http://ucsusa.org/scientific_integrity/solutions/big_picture_solutions/federal-science-and-the.html; and Rena Steinzor, Wendy Wagner, and Matthew Shudtz, *Saving Science from Politics: Nine Essential Reforms of the Legal System*, Center for Progressive Reform, July 2008, http://www.progressivereform.org/articles/SavingScience805.pdf.

[117] On January 30, 2009, President Obama rescinded orders, rules, regulations, guidelines, and policies implementing or enforcing Executive Order 13422 (Executive Order 13497, "Revocation of Certain Executive Orders Concerning Regulatory Planning and Review," 74 *Federal Register* 6113, February 4, 2009).

---

strengthening the Office of Special Counsel;[118] requiring that scientific studies used to inform regulatory policy be disclosed and docketed prior to the decision-making process; reforming agency communication and media policies;[119] and providing the public with both the scientific results or analysis used in policymaking and the ability to include a minority report if there are any significant dissenting scientific evidence or opinions.[120]

Some organizations have suggested that the Obama Administration also address the use of science in regulatory policy, including explicitly differentiating among questions that involve scientific judgments and questions that involve judgments about economics, ethics, and other matters of policy; and develop guidelines on when to consult advisory panels on scientific questions, how to appoint them, how they should operate, and how to deal with conflicts of interest.[121]

Obama Administration

Shortly after taking office, President Obama issued a memorandum for the heads of executive departments and agencies on the subject of scientific integrity. In the memorandum, the President articulated his view of the importance of ensuring scientific integrity; identified several overarching principles; charged the OSTP Director with ensuring "the highest level of scientific integrity in all aspects of the Executive Branch's involvement with scientific and technological processes;" required the Director to confer with heads of executive departments and agencies, the OMB, and other offices within the EOP in the development of a plan to achieve the identified principles; and directed the OSTP Director to develop recommendations for presidential action to guarantee scientific integrity throughout the Executive Branch.[122]

OSTP Director Holdren subsequently issued a memorandum to the heads of executive departments and agencies providing further guidance on implementing the Administration's policies on scientific integrity. Director Holdren's memorandum provided principles in four broad areas: foundations of scientific integrity, public communications, use of federal advisory committees, and professional development of government scientists and engineers. In a separate section addressing implementation, Director Holdren stated that OMB would be issuing guidance to OMB staff regarding standards to be applied to the review of testimony on scientific issues prepared for presentation to Congress. He also noted that "the scope of an agency's scientific

---

[118] The Office of Special Counsel is an independent agency that receives allegations of prohibited personnel practices, investigates such allegations, and conducts investigations of possible prohibited personnel practices on its own initiative, absent any allegation. For more information, CRS Report RL33918, *The Whistleblower Protection Act: An Overview*, by L. Paige Whitaker.

[119] For a discussion of this issue on an agency-specific basis, see Union of Concerned Scientists, *Freedom to Speak? A Report Card on Federal Agency Media Policies*, 2008, http://www.ucsusa.org/assets/documents/scientific_integrity/ Freedom-to-Speak.pdf.

[120] Union of Concerned Scientists, *Federal Science and the Public Good: Securing the Integrity of Science in Policy Making*, February 2008, http://ucsusa.org/scientific_integrity/solutions/big_picture_solutions/federal-science-and-the.html; and Rena Steinzor, Wendy Wagner, and Matthew Shudtz, *Saving Science from Politics: Nine Essential Reforms of the Legal System*, Center for Progressive Reform, July 2008, http://www.progressivereform.org/articles/ SavingScience805.pdf.

[121] Bipartisan Policy Center, *Science for Policy Project*, Interim Report, March 10, 2009, http://www.bipartisanpolicy.org/ht/a/GetDocumentAction/i/9982.

[122] President Barack Obama, *Memorandum for the Heads of Executive Departments and Agencies, Subject: Scientific Integrity*, Washington, DC, March 9, 2009, http://www.whitehouse.gov/the_press_office/Memorandum-for-the-Heads-of-Executive-Departments-and-Agencies-3-9-09/.

---

work and its relationship to the mission of each department or agency may necessitate distinct mechanisms be used by each to implement this guidance." [123]

The OSTP reviewed the guidelines developed by each agency to ensure consistency with the guidance provided in President Obama's original memorandum. [124] According to OSTP, some departments have decided to develop policies that will apply broadly to a number of their component agencies. The OSTP has also stated that individual agencies covered by their departments' policies may develop their own policies with additional elements specific to their missions. [125] According to Director Holdren, as of April 6, 2012, eighteen federal agencies had finalized their policies. [126] Several others have subsequently released final or draft policies. [127]

Some policymakers have asserted that the Obama Administration has failed to protect scientific integrity. For example, in a letter to the OSTP Director, several Members of Congress have alleged scientific misconduct by the Department of the Interior, the Environmental Protection Agency, the Department of Energy, and the Nuclear Regulatory Commission. [128] Among the concerns raised in the letter were data quality, integrity of methodologies and collection of information, agency misrepresentation of the weight of what they asserted were scientific facts, misrepresentation of scientific conclusions in federal courts, and rigorous application of the scientific method.

Congress might opt to influence the direction of the existing executive branch activities, provide oversight of their implementation, or establish alternative reporting mechanisms for issues related to scientific integrity. Congress might establish guidance regarding how agencies should craft and implement scientific integrity policies. Alternatively, Congress might leave establishing and implementing such policies to agency discretion, but instead require regular reporting from agencies regarding scientific integrity issues and the effectiveness of policy enforcement. Finally, Congress could further empower the Inspectors General to address issues of scientific integrity or establish alternative reporting mechanisms, such as a federal ombudsman, to receive complaints regarding scientific integrity issues.

---

[123] John Holdren, *Memorandum for the Heads of Executive Departments and Agencies, Subject: Scientific Integrity*, Office of Science and Technology Policy, Executive Office of the President, Washington, DC, December 17, 2010, http://www.whitehouse.gov/sites/default/files/microsites/ostp/scientific-integrity-memo-12172010.pdf.

[124] Private telephone conversation between CRS and Rachael Leonard, OSTP General Counsel, August 12, 2011.

[125] Rick Weiss, *Scientific Integrity Policies Submitted to OSTP*, Office of Science and Technology Policy, Executive Office of the President, Washington, DC, April 21, 2011, http://www.whitehouse.gov/blog/2011/08/11/scientific-integrity-policies-submitted-ostp.

[126] John Holdren, Director, Office of Science and Technology Policy, OSTP Blog, "Scientific Integrity Policies Released," April 6, 2012, http://www.whitehouse.gov/blog/2012/04/06/scientific-integrity-policies-released.

[127] For example, the Department of Homeland Security issued a directive on scientific integrity on April 12, 2012 (see http://www.dhs.gov/xlibrary/assets/foia/dhs-directive-026-07-scientific-integrity.pdf). The Department of Defense issued an instruction on scientific and engineering integrity on July 26, 2012 (see http://www.dtic.mil/whs/directives/corres/pdf/320020p.pdf).

[128] Letter from Sen. David Vitter, Sen. James Inhofe, and Rep. Darrell Issa to John Holdren, Director, Office of Science and Technology Policy, October 18, 2011.

Stature and Influence of PCAST

As discussed earlier, PCAST advises the President on science, technology, and innovation-related issues. The PCAST's members include individuals from industry, education and research institutions, and other organizations outside the federal government.

Legislative activity has focused less on PCAST than on the NSTC. Some experts in the S&T policy community have asserted that the stature and influence of PCAST has declined as PCAST focused on a narrower set of issues less likely to garner presidential interest.[129] These experts highlight that while President George H.W. Bush held the first PCAST meeting at Camp David and participated in PCAST meetings, Presidents Clinton and George W. Bush only met occasionally for short periods of time with the PCAST chair or committee members.

According to OSTP, through January 2012, President Obama met with PCAST four times during his first three years in office, with each discussion lasting an hour or more. In addition, PCAST co-chairs met with the President and senior EOP officials several times for focused discussions on specific topics that PCAST should undertake for its studies, updates on studies in progress, briefings on completed studies prior to public release, and actions the President could consider in response to PCAST's recommendations.[130]

As a federal advisory committee, PCAST is unusual in that its original executive order states the OSTP Director and one of its members will co-chair it, as opposed to having an independent chair not directly associated with the Administration.[131] This joint-chair approach has continued through succeeding administrations, with the APST co-chairing the Obama Administration PCAST. Federal advisory committees generally do not include Administration staff as committee members or chairs. Administration staff are more commonly included in an ex-officio role.[132] The inclusion of the APST as both member and co-chair may reduce PCAST's ability to provide independent thinking to the White House and may place the APST in an awkward position if PCAST members disagree with White House policy.

Some S&T policy organizations have suggested strengthening PCAST by broadening its mandate, including explicitly national and homeland security issues, enhancing its independence, and increasing its staff significantly.[133] Other suggestions include selecting the chair of PCAST

---

[129] Center for the Study of the Presidency, Study Group on Presidential Science and Technology Personnel Advisory Assets, *"Presidential Leadership to Ensure Science and Technology in Service of National Needs: A Report to the 2008 Candidates,"* Summer 2008 at http://www.thepresidency.org/pubs/science_tech_2008.pdf.

[130] E-mail communication from OSTP General Counsel Rachael Leonard to CRS, January 24, 2012.

[131] Executive Order 12700, "President's Council of Advisors on Science and Technology," 55 *Federal Register* 2219, January 23, 1990.

[132] For example, the Director of the National Science Foundation is an ex-officio member of the National Science Board and the charter of the National Science Advisory Board for Biosecurity allows for non-voting ex-officio representatives of the Executive Office of the President and a number of federal agencies and entities. For more information, see CRS Report R40520, *Federal Advisory Committees: An Overview*, by Wendy Ginsberg.

[133] See for example, Carnegie Commission on Science, Technology, and Government, *Science & Technology and the President* (New York: Carnegie Corporation of New York, October 1988); Henry Kelly, Ivan Oelrich, Steven Aftergood, and Benn H. Tannenbaum, *Flying Blind: The Rise, Fall and Possible Resurrection of Science Policy Advice in the United States* (Washington, DC: Federation of American Scientists, 2004); and Center for the Study of the Presidency, Study Group on Presidential Science and Technology Personnel Advisory Assets, *"Presidential Leadership to Ensure Science and Technology in Service of National Needs: A Report to the 2008 Candidates,"* Summer 2008 at http://www.thepresidency.org/pubs/science_tech_2008.pdf.

solely from its non-Administration members; appointing them to staggering, overlapping terms unrelated to presidential and congressional election cycles; and providing all members with security clearances. The Obama Administration undertakes to provide PCAST members with security clearances.[134]

Some experts in the S&T community have also suggested increasing the number of Presidential advisory committees. For example, they propose advisory committees focused on specific S&T policy issues, for example a Federal-State Science and Technology Council to enhance dialogue with the states, particularly on STEM education.[135] The costs of establishing such new advisory committees may pose a challenge to their creation. In addition, the Federal Advisory Committee Act (P.L. 92-463) requirements regarding justification of any new advisory committee, its membership, and associated ethics rules (including financial disclosure) may complicate establishing new committees and recruiting committee members. As noted above, PCAST has taken on the responsibilities of other more topic-specific advisory committees established in statute.

If Congress would like the President to establish additional Presidential advisory committees—either to address areas not currently covered by PCAST or to address issues currently covered by PCAST but with separate committees focused on a particular area (e.g., nanotechnology, networking and information technology)—it might opt to provided additional funding to OSTP for this purpose.

On November 20, 2008, the members of PCAST in the Bush Administration wrote a letter to the individuals who would succeed them as PCAST members.[136] The letter recommends certain actions to the next PCAST. These recommendations include that PCAST should:

- Play a more active role in advising Congress on issues related to science and technology policy, at the direction of the President, rather than just delivering reports to Congress;

- Consider more congressional activity, where it is needed for the Administration to implement PCAST's recommendations; and

- Increase interactions of PCAST, as a group, with the President, OMB, and CEA.

President Obama stated that PCAST would be "a vigorous external advisory council that will shape my thinking on the scientific aspects of my policy priorities."[137] He announced the new members of PCAST on April 27, 2009,[138] stating,

---

[134] Executive Order 13539, "President's Council of Advisors on Science and Technology," 75 *Federal Register* 21973-21975, April 27, 2010.

[135] Jennifer Sue Bond, Mark Schaefer, David Rejeski, Rodney W. Nichols, *OSTP 2.0: Critical Upgrade: Enhancing Capacity for White House Science and Technology Policymaking: Recommendations for the Next President* (Washington, DC: Woodrow Wilson International Center for Scholars, June 2008) at http://wilsoncenter.org/news/docs/OSTP%20Paper1.pdf; and Center for the Study of the Presidency, Study Group on Presidential Science and Technology Personnel Advisory Assets, "Presidential Leadership to Ensure Science and Technology in Service of National Needs: A Report to the 2008 Candidates," Summer 2008 at http://www.thepresidency.org/pubs/science_tech_2008.pdf.

[136] President's Council of Advisors on Science and Technology, Letter to successors to the President's Council of Advisors on Science and Technology, November 20, 2008 at http://www.ostp.gov/galleries/PCAST/PCAST%20Transition%20Letter%202008-2.pdf.

[137] Dave Rochelson, "The search for knowledge, truth and a greater understanding of the world around us," (continued...)

> We also need to engage the scientific community directly in the work of public policy. And that's why, today, I am announcing the appointment—we are filling out the President's Council of Advisors on Science and Technology, known as PCAST, and I intend to work with them closely. Our co-chairs have already been introduced—Dr. Varmus and Dr. Lander along with John. And this council represents leaders from many scientific disciplines who will bring a diversity of experiences and views. And I will charge PCAST with advising me about national strategies to nurture and sustain a culture of scientific innovation.... [139]

The OSTP asserts that President Obama has increased the role and influence of PCAST by considering and taking action on PCAST recommendations, including:

- Funding a new influenza vaccine manufacturing improvement initiative to shorten the time frame for production of pandemic influenza vaccines, including dedication of the first U.S. cell-based influenza vaccine plant;

- Proposing preparation of an additional 100,000 K-12 STEM teachers by the end of the decade and establishment of an Advanced Research Projects Agency-Education (ARPA-ED);

- Accelerating adoption of Electronic Health Records and developing standards for health information exchange over the Internet, and metadata for Stages 2 and 3 of the electronic health records meaningful use criteria;

- Establishing the Advanced Manufacturing Partnership, including initial funding for new initiatives; and

- Undertaking a Quadrennial Technology Review at the Department of Energy.[140]

The OSTP asserts that during the Obama Administration PCAST has met six times per year compared to 3-4 times per year during the George W. Bush Administration, and that the current PCAST "has met with every major Administration leader in science and technology, including Cabinet-level Secretaries, to gather their views on the topics most useful for PCAST to address, and to discuss implementation of PCAST's recommendations."[141]

In addition, OSTP states that the Obama Administration has provided PCAST with the staff and financial resources necessary to develop reports in a timely fashion for Congress and the Administration. These resources, according to OSTP, have increased the ability of PCAST to provide reports and recommendations. The PCAST released 18 reports during the Bush Administration; through the first three years of the Obama Administration, PCAST has released 14 reports through September 2012.[142] Also, OSTP asserts that the Obama Administration has provided travel support to enable experts to provide advice in-person to PCAST and has ensured

---

(...continued)

Change.gov: The Office of the President-Elect, website, December 20, 2008, at http://change.gov/newsroom/entry/the_search_for_knowledge_truth_and_a_greater_understanding_of_the_world_aro/.

[138] For a list of members, see http://www.ostp.gov/cs/pcast.

[139] The White House, Office of the Press Secretary, Remarks By The President At The National Academy Of Sciences Annual Meeting, April 27, 2009 at http://www.whitehouse.gov/the_press_office/Remarks-by-the-President-at-the-National-Academy-of-Sciences-Annual-Meeting/.

[140] E-mail communication from OSTP General Counsel Rachael Leonard to CRS, January 24, 2012.

[141] Ibid.

[142] http://www.whitehouse.gov/administration/eop/ostp/pcast/docsreports

that most of the current PCAST members have obtained security clearances so that PCAST may undertake studies related to national security.[143]

Activities in the 112th Congress

The 112th Congress has taken a series of legislative actions regarding OSTP and NSTC. Some of these actions have resulted in passage of public laws, while others remain as proposed legislation.

Public Laws

The Department of Defense and Full-Year Continuing Appropriations Act, 2011 (P.L. 112-10), provided FY2011 appropriations of $6.6 million for OSTP. It also contained statutory language prohibiting expenditure of these funds

> to develop, design, plan, promulgate, implement, or execute a bilateral policy, program, order, or contract of any kind to participate, collaborate, or coordinate bilaterally in any way with China or any Chinese-owned company unless such activities are specifically authorized by a law enacted after the date of enactment of this division.

As mentioned above in "OSTP Compliance with Statutory Restrictions on the Use of Appropriated Funds," GAO has asserted that OSTP has violated this provision, while OSTP and DOJ assert the provision cannot bind the President in conduct of constitutional duties.

The Consolidated and Further Continuing Appropriations Act, 2012 (P.L. 112-55), provided FY2012 appropriations of $4.5 million for OSTP. It contains similar statutory language to that found in P.L. 112-10 with the clarification that this prohibition shall not apply to activities which OSTP certifies "pose no risk of resulting in the transfer of technology, data, or other information with national security or economic security implications to China or a Chinese-owned company." The OSTP must submit any such certification to Congress at least 14 days prior to the activity. The conference report accompanying P.L. 112-55 (H.Rept. 112-284) also supports OSTP efforts to coordinate federal STEM education programs and develop a government-wide STEM education strategic plan. Finally, the conference report also encourages OSTP to establish through the NSTC an interagency working group to coordinate federal investments in neuroscience research.

The Continuing Appropriations Resolution, 2013 (P.L. 112-175) extends the statutory language found in P.L. 112-55 through March 27, 2013. It also provides funding for OSTP at the FY2012 rate increased by 0.612% through March 27, 2013.

The National Defense Authorization Act for Fiscal Year 2012 (P.L. 112-81) charges the OSTP Director with establishing an interagency Small Business Innovation Research (SBIR)/Small Business Technology Transfer (STTR) policy committee. The policy committee is to review selected Small Business Innovation Research (SBIR)/Small Business Technology Transfer (STTR) issues and recommend improvements to program effectiveness and efficiency. Similar language was found in the Creating Jobs Through Small Business Innovation Act of 2011, H.R.

---

[143] Ibid.

1425, and the SBIR/STTR Reauthorization Act of 2011, S. 493. The Senate failed to invoke cloture on S. 493 on May 4, 2011.

Proposed Legislation

The Fulfilling the Potential of Women in Academic Science and Engineering Act of 2011 (H.R. 889) would require the OSTP Director to develop a uniform policy charging federal science agencies to convene a regular program of workshops on methods to minimize gender bias. The OSTP Director also would report to Congress regarding the effectiveness of the workshop program and annually publish a list of science and engineering higher education institutions that participate in the workshops. H.R. 889 would also charge the OSTP Director with developing a uniform policy to extend grant durations for federally funded researchers who have caregiving responsibilities and to provide funding for interim technical support for federally funded researchers who take a leave of absence for caregiving responsibilities.

Three bills in the 112th Congress seek to address issues related to rare earth metals, in part, using the NSTC. The Energy Critical Elements Renewal Act of 2011 (H.R. 952) would direct the President to work through OSTP to coordinate federal actions to promote an adequate and stable supply of energy critical elements; identify energy critical elements and establish early warning systems for supply problems of energy critical elements; establish coordination and evaluation mechanism for energy critical element needs; promote and encourage private enterprise in the development of a domestic energy critical elements supply chain; promote and encourage the recycling of energy critical elements; assess the need for and make recommendations concerning the availability and adequacy of the supply of technically trained personnel necessary for energy critical elements research, development, extraction, and industrial production; and report to Congress on these activities. H.R. 952 would also specifically charge the OSTP Director with coordinating through the NSTC federal materials research and development and related activities. The Rare Earths and Critical Materials Revitalization Act of 2011 (H.R. 618), contains similar language regarding the NSTC. The Energy Critical Elements Advancement Act of 2011 (H.R. 2090), would charge the NSTC with reporting to Congress regarding the recycling of energy critical elements, including the logistics, economic viability, and research and development needs; options for the federal government and industry; and an analysis of recycling done in other countries.

The Natural Hazards Risk Reduction Act of 2011 (H.R. 1379 and S. 646) would transfer responsibility for establishing an interagency working group and a national advisory committee on windstorm impact reduction from the OSTP Director to the Director of the National Institute of Standards and Technology. These bills would also charge the OSTP Director with participating in an interagency coordinating committee on natural hazards risk reduction. Finally, these bills would direct the NSTC to report to Congress on the coordination of federal disaster research, development, and technology transfer activities.

Several bills in the 112th Congress would charge OSTP with coordinating responsibilities regarding federal cybersecurity research and development. The Cybersecurity Enhancement Act of 2011 (H.R. 2096 and S. 1152) would direct select federal agencies to work through the NSTC to transmit and triennially maintain a strategic plan for federal cybersecurity and information assurance research and development. These bills would also require the OSTP Director to convene a higher education-industry task force to explore mechanisms for carrying out collaborative research, development, education, and training activities for cybersecurity and report to Congress on its findings and recommendations.

The Cybersecurity Act of 2012 (S. 2105) would charge the OSTP Director, in coordination with the Secretary of Homeland Security, to develop a national cybersecurity research and development plan, support research in secure coding, assess secure coding education in colleges and universities and report such assessment to congressional committees, review cybersecurity test beds and establish a program to award grants to institutions of higher education to establish such test beds, and coordinate cybersecurity research and development with other strategies. Similar language is also found in S. 3414.

The Strengthening and Enhancing Cybersecurity by Using Research, Education, Information, and Technology Act of 2012 (S. 2151 and H.R. 4263) would require the National Science and Technology Council with the assistance of OSTP to develop a five-year cybersecurity strategic plan and implementation roadmap and charge the OSTP Director with transmitting the strategic plan and implementation roadmap to Congress. It also would require the OSTP Director to convene a task force to explore mechanisms for carrying out collaborative research and development activities for cyber-physical systems and report the findings and recommendations of the task force to Congress. Similar language is also found in S. 3342.

The National Hurricane Research Initiative Act of 2011 (H.R. 2258) would charge OSTP, through the NSTC, with coordinating federal activities related to hurricane research as a formal program with a well-defined organizational structure and execution plan.

The Harmful Algal Blooms and Hypoxia Research and Control Amendments Act of 2011 (H.R. 2484) would require the President, through the NSTC, to establish an interagency task force on harmful algal blooms and hypoxia. The task force would coordinate the development of agency budgets regarding federal activities on harmful algal blooms and hypoxia and submit those budgets to OMB. The Oceans and Human Health Reauthorization Act of 2011 (H.R. 3570) would require the NSTC to revise and update the 2007 "Interagency Oceans and Human Health Research Implementation Plan" and submit the updated plan to Congress.

The Quadrennial Energy Review Act of 2011 (S. 1703) would require the Department of Energy to perform a quadrennial energy review. The OSTP Director and the Secretary of Energy would be required to chair a presidentially established interagency working group every four years. The interagency working group would conduct a review to provide an integrated view of national energy objectives and Federal energy policy, including alignment of research programs, incentives, regulations, and partnerships.

The International Science and Technology Cooperation Act of 2012 (H.R. 5916) would require the OSTP Director to establish a body under the NSTC responsible for identifying and coordinating international science and technology cooperation that can strengthen the U.S. science and technology enterprise, improve economic and national security, and support U.S. foreign policy goals. The OSTP Director would report annually to Congress regarding these issues.

H.R. 5952 would require each federal agency to submit and obtain approval from the OSTP Director of guidelines for ensuring and maximizing the quality, objectivity, utility, and integrity of scientific information relied upon by the agency for policy decisions. Such approval would be required before any policy decision could be made subsequent to January 1, 2013. Similar language is also found in the Red Tape Reduction and Small Business Job Creation Act (H.R. 4078).

Appendix. President's Science and Technology Policy Advisers

Table A-1. President's Science and Technology Policy Advisers, Executive Office of the President Agency, Interagency Coordination Organization, and Advisory Committee, 1941-present

President	Advisers with Title(s) (Years in Office)	Executive Office of the President Agency (Year Established)	Interagency Coordination Organization[a] (Year Established)	Advisory Committee (Year Established)
F.D. Roosevelt	**Vannevar Bush**[b] (1941-1945), Director, Office of Scientific Research and Development	Office of Scientific Research and Development (OSRD; 1941)		Science Advisory Board (1933)
Truman	**John Steelman**[b] (1946-1947), Special Assistant to the President (1945-1946); Assistant to the President (1946-1953); Chairman, The President's Scientific Research Board (1946-1947)		The President's Scientific Research Board (1946-1947);[c] Interdepartmental Committee for Scientific Research (1947)[c]	Science Advisory Committee (SAC) of the Office of Defense Mobilization (1946)[c]
	Oliver Buckley[b] (1951-1952); Chair, Science Advisory Committee (SAC)			
	Lee DuBridge[b] (1952-1953), Chair, SAC			
Eisenhower	**Lee DuBridge** (1953-1956), Chair, SAC; Science Adviser to the President	Office of the Special Assistant to the President for Science and Technology (1957)	Federal Council for Science and Technology (FCST) (1959)	SAC (1953-56); President's Science Advisory Committee (PSAC; 1957, replaced SAC).
	Isidor I. Rabi (1956-1957), Chair, SAC; Science Adviser to the President			
	James Killian, Jr. (1957-1959), Special Assistant to the President for Science and Technology; Chair, President's Science Advisory Committee (PSAC)			
	George Kistiakowsky (1959-1961), Special Assistant to the President for Science and Technology; Chair, PSAC			

President	Advisers with Title(s) (Years in Office)	Executive Office of the President Agency (Year Established)	Interagency Coordination Organization[a] (Year Established)	Advisory Committee (Year Established)
Kennedy	**Jerome Wiesner** (1961-1963), Special Assistant to the President for Science and Technology; Director, OST; Chair, FCST; Chair, PSAC	Office of Science and Technology (OST; 1962)	FCST	PSAC
Johnson	**Jerome Wiesner** (1963-1964), Special Assistant to the President for Science and Technology; Director, OST; Chair, FCST; Chair, PSAC	OST	FCST	PSAC
	Donald Hornig (1964-1969), Special Assistant to the President for Science and Technology; Director, OST; Chair, FCST; Chair, PSAC			
Nixon[d]	**Lee DuBridge** (1969-1970), Science Adviser to the President; Director, OST	OST (until 1973, when office abolished)[d]	FCST	PSAC (until 1973, when member resignations were accepted, and no new appointments were made).
	Edward David, Jr. (1970-1973), Science Adviser to the President; Director, OST			
	H. Guyford Stever (1973-1974), Science Adviser to the President; Chair, FCST			
Ford	**H. Guyford Stever** (1974-1977); Science Adviser to the President; Director, Office of Science and Technology Policy (OSTP)	Office of Science and Technology Policy (1976)	Federal Coordinating Council for Science, Engineering, and Technology (FCCSET; 1976, replaced FCST)	Intergovernmental Science, Engineering, and Technology Panel (ISETAP; 1976);[e] President's Council on Science and Technology (PCST; 1976)
Carter	**Frank Press** (1977-1981); Science and Technology Advisor to the President; Director, OSTP; Chair, FCCSET	OSTP	FCCSET dissolved as statutory entity and reestablished under an executive order (1978)	PCST (until 1978, abolished with its functions transferred to President by executive order); ISETAP (in 1978, dissolved as statutory entity and reestablished under an executive order)
Reagan	**George Keyworth, II** (1981-1985), Science Adviser to the President; Director, OSTP	OSTP	FCCSET	White House Science Council (1982; reports to Science Adviser, not President; established by Science Adviser, not executive order)
	William R. Graham (1986 - 1989), Science Adviser to the President; Director, OSTP			

President	Advisers with Title(s) (Years in Office)	Executive Office of the President Agency (Year Established)	Interagency Coordination Organization[a] (Year Established)	Advisory Committee (Year Established)
G.H.W. Bush	**D. Allan Bromley** (1989-1993), Assistant to the President for Science and Technology; Director, OSTP; Chair, PCAST	OSTP	FCCSET	President's Council of Advisors on Science and Technology (PCAST; 1990)
Clinton	**John Gibbons** (1993-1998), Assistant to the President for Science and Technology; Director, OSTP; Co-Chair, PCAST	OSTP	National Science and Technology Council (NSTC; 1993)	PCAST (Name changed to President's Committee of Advisors on Science and Technology; 1993)
	Neal Lane (1998-2001), Assistant to the President for Science and Technology; Director, OSTP; Co-Chair, PCAST			
G.W. Bush	**John Marburger, III** (2001-2009), Science Adviser to the President; Director, OSTP; Co-Chair, PCAST	OSTP	NSTC	PCAST (Name changed back to President's Council of Advisors on Science and Technology; 2001)
Obama	**John P. Holdren** (2009-current), Assistant to the President for Science and Technology; Director, OSTP; Co-Chair, PCAST	OSTP	NSTC	PCAST

Sources: Congressional Research Service. The table is based on information from the following sources: Public Papers of the Presidents (Washington, DC: GPO) with the following volumes were used as references: Dwight D. Eisenhower (1957, 1960); Lyndon B. Johnson (1962, 1966, 1967); Richard M. Nixon (1969, 1970, 1973), Gerald Ford (1976-1977), Jimmy Carter (1977, 1978), Ronald Reagan (1981, 1983, 1986), and George H.W. Bush (1989); Jeffrey K. Stine, A History of Science Policy in the United States, 1940-1985, Report for the House Committee on Science and Technology Task Force on Science Policy, 99th Congress, 2nd session, Committee Print (Washington, DC: GPO, 1986), available at http://ia341018.us.archive.org/2/items/historyofscience00unit/historyofscience00unit.pdf; William T. Golden (ed.), Science Advice to the President (New York: Pergamon Press, 1979); William G. Wells, Science Advice and the Presidency: 1933-1976. Dissertation, School of Government and Business Administration (Washington, DC: George Washington University, 1977); OSTP, "Previous Science Advisers," website at http://www.ostp.gov/cs/about_ostp/ previous_science_advisors, accessed September 19, 2008; Truman Library at http://www.trumanlibrary.org/hstpaper/steelman.htm.; "Lee Alvin DuBridge (Part II) (1901-1993), Interviewed by Judith R. Goodstein," Oral History, February 20, 1981, California Institute of Technology Archives at http://oralhistories.library.caltech.edu/68/01/OH_DuBridge_2.pdf; Nixon Presidential Library Archives, Officials of Administration at http://nixon.archives.gov/thelife/apolitician/thepresident/officialsofadministration.php; John T. Woolley and Gerhard Peters, The American Presidency Project [online], Santa Barbara, CA: University of California (hosted), Gerhard Peters (database) at http://www.presidency.ucsb.edu/; National Archives, "Records of the Office of Science and Technology," webpage at http://www.archives.gov/research/guide-fed-records/groups/359.html. Other sources include Executive Orders 9912, 9913, 10807, 12039, 12881, 12882, 13226; Reorganization Plan No. 1 of 1962; Reorganization Plan No. 2 of 1962; Reorganization Plan No. 1 of 1973; and Reorganization Plan No. 1 of 1977: Executive Order 9912, "Establishing the Interdepartmental Committee on Scientific Research and Development," 12 Federal Register 8799, December 27, 1947 at http://www.presidency.ucsb.edu/ws/index.php?pid=60725; Executive Order 9913, "Terminating the Office of Scientific Research and Development and Providing for the Completion of its Liquidation," 12 Federal Register 8799, December 27, 1947 at http://www.presidency.ucsb.edu/ws/index.php?pid=78155; Executive Order 10807, "Federal Council for Science and Technology, 24 Federal Register 1897, March 17, 1959; Executive Order 12039, "Relating to the Transfer of Certain Science and Technology Policy Functions," 43 Federal Register 8095; February 28, 1978 at http://www.presidency.ucsb.edu/ws/index.php?pid=30416; Executive Order 12881, "Establishment of the National Science and Technology Council," 58 Federal Register 226, November 23, 1993, p. 62491 at http://www.archives.gov/federal-register/executive-orders/pdf/12881.pdf; Executive Order 12882, "Executive Order 12882 - President's Committee of Advisors on Science and Technology," 58 Federal Register 226, November 26, 1993, p. 62493 at http://www.archives.gov/federal-register/executive-orders/pdf/12882.pdf; Executive Order 13226, "President's Council of

Advisors on Science and Technology," 66 Federal Register 192, October 3, 2001, pp. 50523-52524 at http://frwebgate.access.gpo.gov/cgi-bin/getdoc.cgi?dbname=2001_register&docid=fr03oc01-141.pdf; U.S. President (Kennedy), "Special Message to the Congress Transmitting Reorganization Plan 2 of 1962," Public Papers of the Presidents of the United States: John F. Kennedy, 1962, March 29, 1962, at http://www.presidency.ucsb.edu/ws/index.php?pid=24601&st=Reorganization+Plan+No.+2+of+1962&st1=; U.S. President (Nixon), "Message to the Congress Transmitting Reorganization Plan 1 of 1973 Restructuring the Executive Office of the President," Public Papers of the Presidents of the United States: Richard M. Nixon, January 26, 1973, at http://www.presidency.ucsb.edu/ws/index.php?pid=3819&st=Reorganization+Plan+No.+1+of+1973&st1=; U.S. President (Carter), "Executive Office of the President Message to the Congress Transmitting Reorganization Plan No. 1 of 1977," Public Papers of the Presidents of the United States: Jimmy Carter, July 15, 1977, at http://www.presidency.ucsb.edu/ws/index.php?pid=7809&st=Reorganization+Plan+No.+1+of+1977&st1=; Executive Order 13539, "President's Council of Advisors on Science and Technology," 75 Federal Register 21973-21975, April 27, 2010, http://edocket.access.gpo.gov/2010/pdf/2010-9796.pdf.

Notes: The science advisers may have additional titles not represented in this table. In recent times, the hierarchy of assistants to the President within the White House Office is as follows, going from high to low: Assistant to the President, Deputy Assistant to the President, Special Assistant to the President. (National Archives and Records Administration, The United States Government Manual 2007-2008 (Washington, DC: GPO, 2007) at http://www.gpoaccess.gov/gmanual/browse-gm-07.html.)

a.   President Theodore Roosevelt appointed the Committee on the Organization of Scientific Work to assess the central organization of government scientific bureaus (agencies) with a focus on eliminating duplication.

b.   Opinions differ on who is the first presidential science adviser. During the George W. Bush Administration, the OSTP website stated Oliver Buckley was the first science advisor, and did not include either Vannevar Bush or John Steelman in its list of presidential science advisors. Others believe the latter two individuals were presidential science advisers as well. As OSRD Director, Vannevar Bush, submitted a report, Science: The Endless Frontier, to the President Franklin Roosevelt Administration that is the foundation for today's federal S&T policy. President Truman asked that John Steelman, as Director of War Mobilization and Reconversion in the EOP, chair a Presidential Scientific Research Board that was to make recommendations on how to enhance coordination and efficiency of federal R&D. Once this report was released, President Truman asked Steelman, a Presidential Assistant, to act as a liaison between the President and the newly formed Interdepartmental Committee on Scientific Research and Development. Buckley, DuBridge, and Rabi were all Chairs of the Science Advisory Committee and as such, were given the title of Presidential science advisers. For more discussion of this issue, see "Oral History Interview with William T. Golden" at http://www.trumanlibrary.org/oralhist/goldenw.htm.

c.   For an understanding of the charges to the different scientific advisory boards and committees, see "Letter to the Chairman, Science Advisory Committee" at http://trumanlibrary.org/publicpapers/viewpapers.php?pid=301; executive order establishing the President's Scientific Research Board, available at http://www.trumanlibrary.org/executiveorders/index.php?pid=467; and the Interdepartmental Committee for Scientific Research, available at http://www.trumanlibrary.org/publicpapers/index.php?pid=1847&st=&st1=.

d.   On January 26, 1973, as part of a reorganization plan, the Office of Science and Technology within the Executive Office of the President was abolished. All of its duties, including that of Science Adviser, were transferred to the National Science Foundation (NSF). As a result, the NSF Director became the Science Adviser. For more details, see http://www.presidency.ucsb.edu/ws/index.php?pid=3819&st=&st1=.

e.   ISETAP members included the OSTP Director, NSF Director, and state, local, and regional officials.

Author Contact Information

John F. Sargent Jr.
Specialist in Science and Technology Policy
jsargent@crs.loc.gov, 7-9147

Dana A. Shea
Specialist in Science and Technology Policy
dshea@crs.loc.gov, 7-6844

www.ingramcontent.com/pod-product-compliance
Lightning Source LLC
Chambersburg PA
CBHW081231170526
45165CB00009B/3038